Abundant Sense

Abundant Sense

Rahim

-Selected Dohas-

CHANDAN SINHA

Published by Westland Books, a division of Nasadiya Technologies Private Limited, in 2025

No. 269/2B, First Floor, 'Irai Arul', Vimalraj Street, Nethaji Nagar, Alapakkam Main Road, Maduravoyal, Chennai 600095

Westland and the Westland logo are the trademarks of Nasadiya Technologies Private Limited, or its affiliates.

ISBN: 9789360454241

10 9 8 7 6 5 4 3 2 1

Typeset by Ashutosh Jha

Printed at Thomson Press (India) Ltd

For Nandita,
always by my side

Contents

Foreword

Ram Chandra Shukla, the doyen of Hindi literary history and criticism, said that Rahim is as popular and respected amongst Hindi-speaking people as Tulsidas. He attributed this popularity to Rahim's sensitivity to poignant moments in everyday life, and his capacity to articulate them in a refined yet accessible poetic idiom.

As a poetic form, the doha presents a formidable challenge due to its strict discipline of metre and rhyme. Rahim himself underlines this challenge through a telling metaphor:

दीरघ दोहा अरथ के आखर थोरे आहिं।
ज्यों रहीम नट कुंडली, सिमटि कूद चढ़ि जाहिं॥

Chandan Sinha renders it beautifully within these pages, meeting the additional challenge of maintaining the rhyme:

Couplets comprise a few letters but hold abundant sense;
As the crouching acrobat, Rahim, springs atop the fence.

Rahim's metaphors come from everyday life. Born into the top elite of his time, he experienced the highs and lows of both palace intrigues and the battlefield. What makes him remarkable is his keen observation of and sensitivity to the life beyond his own privileged background. His social location gave him access to one aspect of life, and the other he earned through poetic efforts, earning deep insights into human nature and condition. That could be why his words spontaneously leap to the mind in moments of emotion, whether exhilaration or distress.

Far from being the merely didactic utterances of a moralist, Rahim's couplets are repositories of empathy coupled with a great sense of irony. It is ironic then that Rahim's couplets are generally included in our school and college curricula as some sort of aid to Moral Science (whatever that means).

Rahim was not merely a product of his times—he was one of its creators. His period was witnessing not only the making of a composite culture, but also the emergence of a new bold idea of Indian civilisation. And yet, the statecraft and policies adopted by Akbar, the patron of Rahim, ought to be seen as the natural and positive outcome of the cultural processes that took place in the centuries preceding him. These processes led to the emergence of a public sphere of Bhakti, or devotion, (which I have discussed in some detail in my own work, *Kabir, Kabir: The Life and Work of the Early Modern Poet–Philosopher*) and a generally ecumenical ethos in culture resulting in new creative idioms in areas ranging from architecture to poetry and philosophical reflection.

Rahim composed a number of poems celebrating Hindu gods and beliefs, but it made him no less Muslim. In the 'new' civilisation of early modern India, creative expression was able to flourish and be accepted without being subjected to religious and doctrinaire straitjackets. Rahim and many others could pursue their own religious faith systems in their day-to-day life, while feeling at liberty to transcend it in their poetic moments. Their ethos recognised the value of 'this and that' in everyday life as well as in the meta narratives of society, state and governance. Rahim, a believing Muslim, could thus unhesitatingly poetically celebrate Hindu gods. He was not forced to choose either this *or* that, he and his times could feel at ease with this *and* that.

Such was the mizāj-i zamāna, the spirit of the age, to borrow an expression from Abu'l Fazl.

This ease born of self-confidence suffered a grievous blow due to colonial intervention in Indian history. It is no one's case that everything was hunky-dory in pre-British India. The region had grave problems of its own making. In fact, to attribute everything negative in the self to some 'other' is in itself symptomatic of a lack of self-confidence. What to talk of solving anything at all when we are not even capable of creating our own problems! Fortunately, that was not, and is not, the case with Indians.

These days, there is a lot of talk of decolonising the Indian mind, but that quest must not lead to an elusive search for that variant of 'purity' which denies or denigrates the civilisational innovations of early modern India, which made voices like Rahim's possible. Such a denial and denigration would be a medicine much worse than the malady of colonisation.

Herein lies the importance of this wonderful translation of Rahim's poetry. To my mind, besides being the translator's personal tribute to the poet, this book is also an invitation to reflect on and draw the right lessons from Rahim's poetry and its historical context. A well-written, scholarly introduction by the translator is very helpful in this matter. It also gives the reader a fair idea of academic discussions on Rahim and the doha form.

Translating any of the early modern Indian poets is a great challenge due not only to great linguistic changes over the centuries, but also subtle and not so subtle shifts in poetic idiom and, in fact, in the sensibility itself. A contemporary reader, even if quite at ease with the source language (whatever it may be) finds it difficult to comprehend the various expressions of these poets.

The challenge faced by the English translator is naturally much more onerous. In fact, a translator is expected—almost like an acrobat—to maintain the delicate balance between the integrity of the original and the translation. They must preserve in the target language something of the nature of the source, even while making it accessible to an audience in that other language. They must resist the temptation to earn instant popularity by making the translation too easily consumable. Many translators unable or unwilling to resist this temptation end up presenting twentieth- and twenty-first-century Americanised adaptations as translations of a fifteenth- or sixteenth-century Indian poet.

Admirably, Chandan Sinha resists any such temptation. Just as in his translations of Kabir, here too he preserves the integrity of the original. Once again, he successfully meets the challenge of translating the doha form without compromising its defining characteristic—the rhyme. In his introduction, Sinha throws some light on the nature and metre of the doha and the difficulties he faced in maintaining the rhyme in translation.

Some couplets of Rahim have been previously translated here and there; this volume presents a substantial body of his couplets in English translation for the first time. While preserving the brevity and wit of the original, the translator has provided an explanation of the context with every couplet. For example, the second doha in the section on 'Friends and Friendship' carries the explanation, 'While going through a difficult time, Rahim points to his own disempowered condition and warns his friends that they should not expect anything from him. Although known for his large-heartedness, in his present circumstances he has nothing to offer them; indeed, he is himself dependent on others. With this frank declaration of penury, perhaps Rahim also seeks to find out who among his circle of friends will stay by him when he is down and out.'

Chandan Sinha deserves our gratitude for his labour of love—these excellent translations.

Purushottam Agrawal

Writer, critic and intellectual historian; former professor, JNU; former member, UPSC

Introduction

Off the erstwhile Grand Trunk Road, now known as Delhi's Mathura Road, close to the dargah of Nizamuddin Aulia, stands a mausoleum in red sandstone partially clad in gleaming marble. This is the tomb of Abdur Rahim Khan-i-Khanan, built by him for his wife Mah Banu. Abdur Rahim also lies there, next to his wife. This relatively small but beautifully proportioned structure has been subject to the depredations of looters, distinguished and undistinguished, since the mid-1800s. Shuja-ud-Daulah was the first to inflict extensive damage on the building during the construction of his father Safdar Jung's tomb in 1754. Saved for long from collapsing upon itself, but not from the attentions of petty vandals, by the Archaeological Survey of India, the mausoleum was restored with the help of the Agha Khan Trust, with additional funding by corporate donors. The work began in 2015 and was completed in 2020. After the extensive conservation project, with the marble partially restored and its other ornaments in sandstone conserved and refurbished, the grandeur of the original has become apparent.

This mausoleum is the principal memorial to one of the most remarkable personalities to tread upon our land—warrior, general, administrator, leading minister of the empire, scholar, polyglot, translator and poet.[1] It is also a memorial to a man who weathered extreme vicissitudes of fortune.

One of the minor changes brought in by the recent restoration is the placement of tall sandstone plaques in each of the four alcoves at the base of the monument. Upon each vertical plaque are engraved two dohas, couplets, by Rahim in Brajbhasha. Although this is but a minuscule modification in the scheme of the monument, the placement of these plaques marks a significant shift. It is an acknowledgement of the fact that the minister,

---

1 If this description of Abdur Rahim is deemed hyperbolic, consider the title of a recent book to which have contributed some of the most eminent scholars of the subject: *Celebrating Abdur Rahim Khan-i-Khana: Statesman, Courtier, Soldier, Poet, Linguist, Humanitarian, Patron*, edited by Shakeel Hussain and Deeti Ray. Ahmedabad: Mapin Publishing, 2017.

general and closest confidante of Akbar, and also for a time of Jahangir, is now remembered more widely as a poet. The first sentence on a plaque near the entrance is meant to be a summary introduction to Abdur Rahim: 'Rahim was famous for his dohas and Persian translation of the Ramayana.'[2] As we shall see, there was much more to Abdur Rahim Khan-i-Khanan's life and accomplishments, even as a poet.

Life and Persona

Although the exact date of Abdur Rahim's birth is unclear,[3] he was born in December 1556 to Bairam Khan, Khan-i-Khanan[4] to Humayun and Akbar, and the younger daughter of Jamal Khan Mewati, the Nawab of Mewat. In January 1561, when Abdur Rahim was four years old, Bairam Khan was murdered by some Afghans near Patan in Gujarat while he was on his way to Mecca. Emperor Akbar

2 Only the first half of the summary is accurate. Not Rahim but the atelier attached to his library produced several illustrated translations of the Ramayana.

3 See Devi Prasad, Munshi. *Khanakhanan Nama*, edited by Jaswant Singh. New Delhi: Rupa Publications, 2006, p. 6.

4 The highest position in the imperial court after the Emperor, except for the princes.

took Bairam Khan's family under his wing, especially caring for Abdur Rahim's upbringing. The emperor appointed Mulla Muhammad Amin Andjani, an eminent scholar, as Abdur Rahim's ataliq or tutor. The child received an education befitting his lineage and nobility: the knowledge and skills of a courtier, warrior, writer, poet and linguist. 'He acquired proficiency in various languages, such as Arabic, Persian, Turkish and Sanskrit, as well as Hindavi, his mother tongue. He developed a refined taste and sensibility for poetry in different languages' (Siddiqui 2017, 58). The atmosphere of the imperial court, where luminaries of diverse fields were welcomed and supported by the Emperor, also nurtured Abdur Rahim.

Akbar's attention was not to be in vain. His protégé grew up to be adept in the use of arms and was an exceptional horseman; poets praised in verse his many accomplishments.[5] Abdur Rahim's reputation was founded on the display of his courage and skill on the battlefields of Gujarat and Sind. The following doha written by him may well apply to his reputation:

---

5 See Bhati, Deshraj Singh. *Rahim Granthavali*. New Delhi: Naman Prakashan, 2011, pp. 3–4.

साधु सराहै साधुता, जती जोखिता जान ॥
रहिमन सांचे सूर को, बैरी करै बखान ॥

Pious folk applaud piety, yogis unworldly ways;
Rahiman, on the truly brave enemies shower praise.

Abdur Rahim emerged as a fearless leader of men, a master tactician and strategist. That this was how he was seen during his lifetime is affirmed by the fact that, in *Ma'asir-ul-Rahimi* (1616), Rahim's biographer Nihawandi refers to him most often as 'the General'.

At the age of sixteen, Rahim accompanied Akbar in his conquest of Gujarat, and for his bravery in battle received from the Emperor the jagir of Patan, the place where he lost his father—an ironic detail from the life of the general-poet. Thereafter, during Akbar's long reign, Rahim's rise was steady and unmatched. In 1575, within two years of the receipt of the jagir of Patan, Akbar appointed Abdur Rahim Khan the governor of Gujarat. He was only nineteen at the time. Rahim was then sent to take charge of the battle against the Rana of Mewar, where he spent two years.

Rahim was married to Mah Bano, the daughter of Anga, the emperor's foster mother, and thus entered a small, powerful circle close to the royal family. He was successively appointed Mirza, Mir Arz, the governor of Ajmer, and at the age of twenty-six, ataliq, or tutor, to Prince Salim, who would succeed Akbar to the throne as Jahangir.

At twenty-eight, after his brilliant military victory in Gujarat, Akbar conferred upon Abdur Rahim the title and position of Khan-i-Khanan, which Rahim's father had also held, as well as a mansabdari of 5,000 men. A few years later, upon the death of Raja Todar Mal, Abdur Rahim was also made Vakil of the empire. He was given charge of the Mughal campaign in the Deccan, where he spent a tumultuous thirty years. By the time he was fifty years old, Rahim—long acknowledged as one of the Navratnas, nine jewels, of Akbar's court—had come to hold the highest positions in the imperial system.

Abdur Rahim had a great love of learning and poetry. An avid collector of books, he continued to accumulate them throughout his career. Nihavandi records that Abdur Rahim's library, with its 'tens of thousands of books', moved with him to the different places where he spent time. His first library was at

Ahmedabad. It later shifted with him to Sironj in Malwa, and then moved to Burhanpur, Rahim's base in the Deccan, where it stayed for the next twenty years (Chander Shekhar 2017, 102). The library attracted not only scholars and poets of repute, but also craftsmen who dealt in the making and preservation of books. Over time, it was inevitable that an atelier, or workshop, should develop around the library, and indeed it did. The epilogue of the *Ma'asir-i-Rahimi* contains the biographies of 191 persons who worked for Abdur Rahim. This large number includes not only scholars, learned men, nobles and poets, but also artists, calligraphers, painters and book binders (Orthmann 2017, 76). In this atelier were preserved a number of invaluable books that the Khan-i-Khanan collected with great effort and at considerable expense, such as the *Khamsa-i-Khusro* (Chander Shekhar 2017, 103).

Apart from being famous as a general, a poet and a man of learning, Abdur Rahim was renowned for his generosity and patronage.[6] His reputation drew the unfortunate and the alms seekers to his door and

---

6 For stories about Abdur Rahim Khan-i-Khanan's generosity, see Devi Prasad, Munshi (2006, pp. 148–150) and Yajnik, Mayashankar (1928, pp. 68–72).

penurious poets and scholars to his court. Rahim was also renowned for his humility. It came to be widely known that, while giving alms to the poor and gifts to those around him, he would always lower his eyes. Puzzled by this, the poet Gang purportedly sent him a question in the form of a doha:

सीखे कहां नवाबजू, ऐसी देनी दैन।
ज्यों ज्यों कर ऊंचो करो, त्यों त्यों नीचे नैन॥

Esteemed Nawab, where did you learn to give
gifts in this way?
Even as you raise your hands to give, your eyes
drop away.

To which Rahim responded with the following couplet:

देनहार कोउ और है, भेजत सो दिन रैन।
लोग भरम हम पै धरें, याते नीचे नैन॥

The benefactor is someone else who sends night and day;
Yet people hold me responsible, therefore the lowered gaze.

With Akbar's death and the ascension of Jahangir to the imperial throne in 1605, Abdur Rahim's fortunes began to change. Given his position and importance in Akbar's court, it was inevitable that he would be drawn into the internecine struggle for succession to the throne. Further, his seeming lack of success in the complicated arena of the Deccan eroded his position in court. The loss of two sons, the ire—first, of Jahangir and then of his sons—followed by the killing of two young grandsons, and finally the beheading of another son were some of the depths of despair and sorrow through which Abdur Rahim passed. At the age of seventy, he did regain Emperor Jahnagir's favour, and once again became the Khan-i-Khanan. But by then Rahim had lost much that could never be retrieved. Within two years, in 1627, he passed away.

Emergence of a Poet

In Rahim's biography *Ma'asir-i-Rahimi*, which he had himself commissioned, Abul Baqi Nihavandi has recorded in thriftless detail the protagonist's life and work. He notes that Rahim wrote in Persian, Arabic, Turkic and Hindi and patronised scholars and poets. Not very many of Rahim's Persian poems survive, while those in Arabic and Turkish are yet to be identified (Lefèvre 2014, 94). The surviving poems in Persian, as copied in *Ma'asir-i-Rahimi* and recorded elsewhere, belong to the shorter formats that Rahim favoured in his Hindavi poetry.

Nihavandi mentions that Abdur Rahim wrote also in Hindi, but he does not include any of these poems in the *Ma'asir-i-Rahimi*. He wrote, 'He uses Rahim as his pen-name. He has composed brilliant verses in Hindi, Turki and Arabic. In Hindi, he has effected a miracle. He has such weighty and delightful verses in the language that none of the poets of the age can match him' (Sharma 2017, 95). The Khan-i-Khanan's use of the pen-name 'Rahim' is also mentioned in the *Ma'asir-ul-Umra* (Devi Prasad 2006, 145)—a who's who of the nobles of the period. That Rahim wrote in Hindi is also mentioned in two 'dictionaries of Mughal nobles', the mid-seventeenth century *Dhakhiratul Khawanin* and the mid-eighteenth century *Ma'asir-ul-Umra*. T.C.A. Raghavan notes, 'All these Persian sources mention Rahim's patronage of literature and also that he composed poetry in Arabic, Persian and Hindi, although no examples are cited of his verses in Hindi' (2017, 253). In the mid-eighteenth century, however, we come across a verse from *Kavyanirnay* (*Critical Perspective on Literature*, 1746) by Bhikharidas, a renowned Braj scholar and theoretician, mentioning Rahim. In the verse, Bhikharidas identified the 'purposes of poetry':

Some acquire religious merit, such as the spiritual masters Tulsi and Sur.
Others seek wealth, in the manner of Keshavdas, Bhushan, and Birbal.
There are the Rahims and Raskhans who concern themselves with fame alone.
Says [Bhikhari] Das, Discussing poetry is in every case pleasing to scholars.

(Busch 2014, 118)

Although Bhikharidas did not record any of Rahim's Braj poetry, by mentioning him in the same breath as Tulsidas, Surdas, Keshavdas and Bhushan, he clearly indicated that Rahim belonged in the highest ranks of Braj poets.[7] The above excerpt also

7 The ranking of poets had begun well before the rankings of songs/records ushered in by the gramophone and the jukebox age. Although around 1922–23 the magisterial Ram Chandra Shukla had relegated Rahim, along with twenty-one other poets, to the rank of minor poets of the Bhakti period (Trivedi 2019b, p. 124), his stock has continued to rise ever since. Mayashankar

reveals that Birbal, another of the nine jewels of Akbar's court, was a highly regarded Braj poet. Busch points out that Badauni and Shah Nawaz Khan—two Persian historians of the royal court—noted that Akbar had bestowed upon Birbal the title of 'Kavirai' (King of Poets). However, these two Persian historians had nothing to say about Birbal's poetry, nor did they record even a few verses by him (Busch 2014, 138). Nihavandi was new to this land of multiple languages, knew little or no Braj *and* was convinced of the superiority of his mother tongue. It would then be scarcely surprising if he did not record any of Rahim's Hindi poems.

However, that Abdur Rahim wrote extensively in Hindi is attested to by the numerous panegyrics to him by some of the most prominent Hindi poets of the age. To be sure, Rahim's legendary generosity attracted poets and scholars to his court, yet so did his attractive personality and his literary accomplishments. We find that a host of major

---

Yajnik pulled him up considerably by stating that, 'among all the poets Rahim ranks if not among the nine jewels then certainly among the top forty jewels of literature' (1928, p. 14). By 1986, Ram Swarup Chaturvedi had placed Rahim among the top six poets of the Bhakti period (Trivedi, 2019b, p. 124).

poets of his time, such as Keshavdas, Gang, Harinath and Mandan, wrote about Rahim and his many outstanding qualities—the distinction of his lineage, courage as a warrior, fairness as an administrator, brilliance as a poet, liberality as a patron and so on.[8] Their exalted praise of the Khan-i-Khanan bore fruit. As per Nihavandi's record, Rahim 'bestowed on Hindi poets, tenfold of the rewards and favours that he did on Persian poets, and compared to the number of verses that Hindi poets have composed for him, Persian poets have not composed a tenth of it' (Sharma 2017, 95).

Raghavan traces the emergence of the poet Rahim from the shadows of Rahim the Khan-i-Khanan in the context of Hindi emerging as a language in its own right. He points out that, almost until the end of the nineteenth century, Rahim does not feature at all in the anthologies of Hindi poetry, or in the lists of poets and writers and the histories of Hindi literature that appeared in either English, French or Hindi. The absence of Rahim's dohas from the anthologies is

8 For more about the poets and their verses in praise of Rahim, see Mishra and Rajneesh, (2005, pp. 47–58).

strange, given their popularity among the people in general.[9]

Raghavan notes that the first mention of Rahim in an anthology of Hindi poets is found in Shiv Singh Sengor's *Shiv Singh Saroj*, published in 1887; it carries a short but comprehensive introduction to Rahim and his work in Sanskrit and Braj Bhasha. For a full-length treatment of Abdur Rahim and his Sanskrit and Hindi poetry, we have to wait for Munshi Devi Prasad's *Khanakhanan Nama*, published in 1906. *Mishra Bandhu Vinod* (1913), an anthology of Hindi poetry, introduced Rahim as a devotee of Rama and Krishna, perhaps for the first time. The growing interest in Abdur Rahim, especially by noted members of the Nagari Pracharini Sabha of Varanasi—devoted to the development and spread of Hindi—resulted in the discovery of new texts by him. The publication of Brij Ratna Das's *Rahiman Vilas* (1923 & 1929) and Mayashankar Yajnik's *Rahim Ratnavali* (1928) marked two important developments: first, the presentation of almost all the known dohas of Rahim (289 in *Rahiman Vilas*, the numbers of which have not increased since);

---

9 For an extensive discussion of this topic, see 'Afterlife: Rahim and Rahiman' in Raghavan, T.C.A. (2017, Ch. 6).

and, second, the shift from a historical to a literary exploration of Rahim and his Hindi poetry. Raghavan also notes that the publication of a series of books on Rahim in the 1920s consolidated his position as a prominent Hindi poet and a representative of the composite Indian culture.

As mentioned earlier, Rahim was adept at several languages; he wrote in Persian, Arabic, Turkish, Sanskrit, Braj Bhasha, Awadhi and Khadi Boli. It was his facility with Turkic that enabled him to translate the *Baburnama*. While it is certainly remarkable that Rahim wrote in these many languages with facility, what is equally striking is that his poetry in each of these languages embraced the poetic traditions and conventions, and incorporated the prosodic forms and elements peculiar to each of these languages, including Brajbhasha and Awadhi. As Lefèvre notes, 'Taken as a whole, this [Hindavi] portion of Rahim's oeuvre shows that he had full command over a range of linguistic registers in the Hindavi tradition of court poetry as well as its lyrical imagery and formal conventions' (2014, 97). Despite writing verse that embraced the accepted conventions and forms of poetry, Mayashankar Yajnik very nearly accuses Rahim of lacking depth and not working hard enough to beautify his poems. Yajnik seems to believe that Rahim just wrote down thoughts when they came to him rather than work hard on imagination or ideas, probably because he led a very busy life, embroiled as he was in matters of court, military campaigns and intrigues (1928, 17). Later scholars like Balakrishna Akinchan,[10] however, have praised the scope and form of Rahim's imagination and ideas.

Not only did Abdur Rahim write extensively in several languages, he also experimented with form and metre. As Manager Pandey points out, in Rahim's *Madnashtak*, we find him using a rare combination of Sanskrit and Khadi Boli (2019, 53). Rahim is also credited with writing in a new verse form—barvai. As contemporaries, Abdur Rahim and Tulsidas are said to have been in touch with each other. It is believed that Tulsidas liked some barvai verses that Rahim sent him so much that they became the inspiration for his short but beautiful *Barvai Ramayan*. This is attested to by Baba Benimadhav Das, one of Tulsidas's principal disciples, in his biography of his guru, *Gusain Charit*, published seven years after Tulsidas's death. The work includes this doha (Yajnik 1928, 46):

---

10 See Bhati, Deshraj Singh (2011, p. 41).

कवि रहीम बरवे रचे, पठये मुनिवर पास।
लखि तेइ सुन्दर छन्द में, रचना कियेउ प्रकास॥

The poet Rahim wrote barvai and sent them to the sage
Who composed a new poem in the winsome form of verse.

However, due to the absence of specific textual evidence, some scholars such as Corinne Lefèvre reject the idea that Rahim patronised Braj Bhasha poets such as Kesavadas and Gang or that he influenced Tulsidas's *Barvai Ramayan* (2014, 84–85).

Experimentation aside, Rahim's poetry in Hindi also displays his facility with several verse forms and genres. There has long been a tendency to characterise him principally as either a Bhakti or Riti or Niti poet. However, the basis for such pigeonholing is shaky, not only because Rahim wrote brilliant poetry of all three kinds but also because, whether in terms of numbers or impact, it would be difficult to establish the dominance of one over the others. In his dohas, too, we find representations of Bhakti, Riti and Niti traditions. Both Bhakti and Shringar, themes and elements of romantic love and beauty, are present in his poems such as *Madanashtak* as well as in some barvais and dohas.

Using both Sanskrit and Persian, he wrote *Kheta-Kautukam*, which describes the effects of the nine planets on the twelve houses of a horoscope—an example of his knowledge of astrology. Rahim's *Nagarshobha*, made up of 142 dohas, depicts women of thirty-five castes, and summarises their chief attributes and attractions. Though shringar is the chief rasa in this work, *Nagarshobha* is also remarkable as a unique sociological study of the women of the era (Trivedi 2017-2, 129). *Barvai Nayika Bhed*, comprising 116 barvais and distinguishing different kinds of lovers—female and male—is another composition replete with shringar rasa; it too would fall within the purview of Riti poetry.

A little further along, we will examine in some detail Rahim's treatment of Niti in his dohas. At this juncture, we may do well to heed Harish Trivedi's words, 'It would be rare to find a poet in Hindi who is seen to belong equally to all three categories and held in equal esteem in Bhakti, Riti and Niti poetry. Yet if we examine closely Rahim proves to be neither a Bhakti poet nor a Riti and Niti poet in the general and popular sense' (2019b, 124).

Bhakti

Several scholars and commentators have referred to Rahim as a poet of Bhakti, in the tradition of Namdev, Kabir, Surdas and Ravidas. This view appears to be based on a section of Rahim's poetry that includes Sanskrit verses, the *Madanashtak*, a selection of barvai celebrating the god Krishna and dohas that include references to Hindu deities and stories from the epics Ramayana and Mahabharata. Rahim has written a significant number of poems that focus on or feature Hindu gods, clear evidence that he had a more than adequate knowledge of the Hindu epics and the Puranas. That such knowledge should make Abdur Rahim a reverent devotee of the gods Krishna or Rama is neither logical nor inevitable. Yet, in the backdrop of nationalism and the effulgent growth of Hindi in the first half of the nineteenth century, Rahim the general and poet was transformed into Rahim the Bhakti poet and Krishna bhakta.

The first major book on Rahim by Munshi Devi Prasad, *Khanakhanan Nama* (1906), is a historical treatment of the subject. Although Abdur Rahim is recognised as a poet, he is firmly, as the title of the book declares, the Khanakhanan. Far from considering Rahim a Bhakti poet, Devi Prasad, unlike later scholars, 'remains circumspect ... about Abdur Rahim's Hindi and Sanskrit poetry: its frequent and pronounced invocation of an obviously Hindu cultural and religious paradigm and the absence of an Islamic "accent"' (Raghavan 2017, 266–67). In the next major work on Rahim, Brij Ratan Das's *Rahiman Vilas* (1923), not only does the author take note of the several Hindu and Bhakti elements of Rahim's poetry, he goes on to say that this 'could only be the work of a person such as Abdul Rahim who despite being the follower of one faith could have such a liberal attitude towards another that he started to *appear* as its devotee' (italics mine) (Raghavan 2017, 269). It looks like, by this time, Rahim had entered the ranks of Bhakti poets.

Apart from the use of subjects, characters and contexts from Hindu religious texts, it was also noted that in Rahim's 'work, [Hindu] Gods and religious ideas are present but there is no contempt for them' (Yajnik 1928, 13). It may, therefore, not be surprising if this also gave a fillip to the belief that he had deep reverence for Hindu deities and religious texts—or even that he had become a devotee of Krishna or Rama. This belief may also have helped in Rahim's recognition as a Hindi poet by the nineteenth-century movement for the development and prioritisation of the language. However, there were also early sceptics of this view. Mayashankar Yajnik, one of the earliest Hindi scholars to study and comment on Rahim's poetry, noted, 'He had peerless reverence for Hindu religion and was a follower of Vaishnavism and a devotee of Shri Krishna—this has also been written *but no evidence for it has been found*' (italics mine) (1928, 14).

Although there is no evidence to indicate how it happened, over time, the notion of Rahim as a Bhakti poet became established, among lay readers, if not among scholars. This idea does not take into account the fact that with the establishment of Persian as the official language of the court, and with the translation into Persian of the epics Mahabharata and Ramayana and their dissemination—the nobility would have been familiar with these works. 'Indo-Persian intellectuals largely viewed the Indian epics as historical and literary materials rather than as religious texts' (Truschke 2015, 6). Of course, a polymath like Rahim would likely have not only read the Persian versions of the epics but also the original texts in Sanskrit.

On the other hand, there is, in fact, enough evidence to show that Abdur Rahim was firm in his faith. For instance, in the historian 'Badauni's estimation, Abdur Rahim stood out as one whose Islamic moorings were strong and immune to the liberal vagaries of the court' (Raghavan 2017, 202). Harish Trivedi has shown most lucidly, with examples from Rahim's Hindi and Sanskrit verses, the contradictions between the perception of the poet as a devotee of Hindu deities and the substance and tenor of some of his writings.[11] Just because Rahim followed tradition and wrote verses based on Hindu religious texts does not make him a devotee. If anything, the fact that he should be considered to be a Krishna bhakta based on his poetry is a testament to Rahim's success as a poet. In this regard, Trivedi's assessment of Rahim is probably the most accurate:

> he harboured in harmony within his heart, two quite distinct possibilities, the one Perso-Muslim and the other Sanskrit-Hindu. And there was consummate compatibility between them rather than conflict and contradiction,

11 See 'Rahim ki Jeevan Drishti' in Trivedi, Harish and Ray, Deeti (eds) (2019b, pp. 124–127).

> perhaps because they were held together by Rahim's poetic imagination, and not by his personal faith (Trivedi 2017, 51).

Ultimately, the poet in Rahim rose above his other characteristics, predilections and passions.

Dohas

A particularly economical verse form, the doha, or couplet, is one of the chief forms used in Bhakti and Riti kaal poetry. A doha comprises two lines that rhyme, with each line made up of twenty-four phonetic units called 'matras'; hence, not all couplets are dohas. Rupert Snell notes that its 'balanced structure makes it [the doha] appropriate for the widest possible array of genres' (2017, 163). Each doha may be a complete poem in itself, or a series of couplets may comprise a longer poem. 'The poet has only a few words to work with and is constrained by a tightly controlled metrical and rhyme scheme. The art of the couplet is to pack a lot of meaning into a tiny vessel' (Busch in Hussain and Ray 2017, 174). In the words of Rahim:

दीरघ दोहा अरथ के, आखर थोरे आहिं।
ज्यों रहीम नट कुंडली, सिमटी कूदि चढ़ि जाहिं॥

Couplets comprise a few letters but hold abundant sense;
As the crouching acrobat, Rahim, springs atop the fence.

A doha conveys a central message usually with the aid of a figure of speech, commonly a simile or a metaphor. Other literary devices, such as alliteration, assonance and onomatopoeia are also deployed. However, it is the 'rhyme-induced surprise', as John Hawley (2020, xi) calls it, at the end of the doha, that seals the impact of the couplet.

To my mind, the surprise caused by rhyme, together with the figure of speech, serves a very important function—it makes the doha memorable. Is it any wonder that, across the northern states of India, the dohas of Kabir, Rahim, Raidas, Bihari and others have been, and continue to be, quoted by generations to make a point, convey a message, to remind or to chide? Metre and rhyme enable the memory to grasp the doha easily. The metre may be what creates the rhythm that carries the sentiment, yet it is the repetition of sound combined with the sudden revelation or surprised recognition of the conveyed message that makes rhyme an effective and integral part of poetry that is easy to remember.

I firmly believe that translations must be as faithful to the original as possible, and agree entirely with Ralph Russell when he says, 'My own general principle is to try to reproduce in translation everything I can which I find in the original—rhythm, assonance, alliteration and even word order where the natural patterns of the word order in the two languages do not preclude this' (Russell 2011, 534). Therefore, I have tried to retain every element of the original doha—words, phrases, context, order of segments and, of course, the meaning—in the translation. The aim is to recreate the clarity of the message of the doha with its original inflections so that Rahim's voice may be heard again.

In the past century or so, in many languages, the importance of rhymed verse and metrical poems, including the couplet, have declined, and free verse has come to hold sway. Perhaps structured verse came to be perceived as a barrier to the democratisation of verse and poetry writing, and the discipline required to create it a burden; consequently, both have been largely abandoned. Free verse, apart from becoming the most popular form among modern poets, has also become the chief vehicle of poetry in translation. However, in my view, translations of structured poetry—in this instance, dohas—without metre and rhyme lose much of the impact of the original. The element of surprise that strikes the reader is lost. Therefore, although difficult to recreate, my attempt has been to translate the dohas in metre and rhyme. Nevertheless, I have not allowed rhyme to take precedence over the message and the meaning sought to be conveyed. The order of segments in a line has been altered occasionally in the interest of clarity. I have not, however, tried to force the rhyme. Hence, there are a few translations that, although metrical, are not in rhyme—not even in 'near-rhyme'. For instance:

जो रहीम करिबो हुतो, ब्रज का इहै हवाल ।
तौ काहे कर पर धरयौ गोबर्धन गोपाल ॥

If, Rahim, this is what you would do to the land of Braj,
Why then raise high Govardhan hill upon
your palm, Gopal?

While translating dohas in metre and rhyme, I have been conscious of a nagging issue: dohas are dense with meaning, often use a figure of speech and have a well-established structure with a fixed metrical length made up of twenty-four matras and two padas, or segments, in each of the two lines in the ratio of 13:11 matras. Hence, a question crops up: when translating them into English in metre and rhyme, is it possible to identify a particular metrical scheme for the doha in translation? The challenge is one of unpacking a number of ideas, concepts or thoughts from one short line in Hindi of twenty-four matras and repackaging them into a line of English in a coherent, pleasing and metrical form.

In the pages that follow, the length of the translations varies from twelve to fifteen syllables; there is one exception—a translation with sixteen syllables in each line. The majority of the translations comprise lines of fourteen syllables each, and each of these lines usually consists of two segments of eight and six syllables respectively. The lines in the dohas translated with twelve, thirteen or fifteen syllables per line also have two parts with the first part of each line being usually longer. Yet, at times, in lines of twelve syllables, the two parts of each line may also be of equal length. I find that in translation dohas with lines of fourteen syllables, with each line made up of two parts of eight and six syllables, respectively, comes closest to replicating the rhythm of the original and may offer the most workable standard. Yet, in view of the varying density of ideas among dohas, settling on this as the only metrical length for dohas in translation would be Procrustean and self-defeating; in a large number of cases, lines of thirteen or even twelve syllables also echo the rhythm of the original equally well. Overall, I have tried to ensure that, apart from the meaning, the sentiment and the voice, the structure of the original doha is also reflected in the translation to the extent that it is possible.

Rahim's Dohas

Rahim was supposed to have authored a Satsai, or collection of seven hundred dohas, an ambition pursued by accomplished poets of the time. It is most doubtful that he did, though. Without gliding into empty speculation on the matter of the Satsai, we must recognise the fact that the number of Rahim's dohas available, and largely agreed upon, hovers around 290. Brij Ratna Das presented the first and probably the most enduring collection of dohas in *Rahiman Vilas*, numbering 289. The number came down to 270 in Mayashankar Yajnik's *Rahim*

Ratnavali. Later, we find that Vidyaniwas Mishra and Govind Rajneesh's *Granthavali* offers 290 dohas, while Deshraj Singh Bhati's *Granthavali* raises the figure to 293. Clearly, the number of dohas added to Rahim's corpus has not grown much, and has certainly not exceeded 300. Nevertheless, considering his body of writing, and his many political, administrative preoccupations as well as personal and social commitments, this collection of dohas is impressive enough for Allison Busch to call Rahim 'the master of the couplet' (2017, 193).

Despite the excellence of Rahim's poetry in other verse forms, his popularity among the public at large undoubtedly rests on his dohas. They have survived in the collective memory, and been passed down the generations over the last five centuries, chiefly through the oral tradition. The charming simplicity of his language—perhaps the most engaging quality of Rahim's dohas—may be one of the key reasons they have endured. Written in Brajbhasha, these dohas use everyday words and common idiom, easy to grasp and relatable. An additional appeal of Rahim's dohas is his knowledge of the world of the common person and his unusual ability to sympathise with them. A glance at the following doha may clarify the point:

कहि रहीम धन बढ़ि घटे, जात धनिन की बात ।
घटै बढै उनको कहा, घास बेंचि जे खात ॥

Rahim, wealth grows or wanes matters to the well-off class;
What is more or less to those who live by selling grass?

Rahim is able to convey that poverty and wealth may also depend upon where we stand, i.e., on our perspective. The growth or decline of wealth is meaningful only to those who possess some. A poor person who struggles for two meals a day would hardly become well-off even if she were to double her money and possessions. As Manager Pandey notes, Rahim is one of the few court poets who wrote about the plight of the poor, highlighting the vulnerability of their predicament. Not only did he draw inspiration from the life of ordinary folk, but he also employed their language in his dohas (2019, 54). This ability to share their world could enable Abdur Rahim Khan-i-Khanan to connect even with a grass-cutter.

The day-to-day experiences of ordinary folk supplied the metaphors that Rahim employed in his dohas; even today they express and evoke shared emotions and beliefs. This quality also strengthens the dohas. Since almost everyone is acquainted with these metaphors, they light up his message. Consider the following doha:

रहिमन अती न कीजिये, गहि रहिये निज कानि ।
सैजन अति फूले तऊ, डार पात की हानि ॥

Rahim says, listen carefully, you must avoid excess;
If the morenga blooms too much, its boughs snap under stress.

The warning to avoid excess in everything and the advice to be moderate is illustrated by the image of the slender branches of a morenga tree cracking under the abundance of the long, thin fruit.

Rahim's metaphors were also drawn from shared traditions and mythology. For instance, to deride both begging and deception, the poet refers to the story of Lord Vishnu tricking the generous King Bali out of his kingdom:

माँगे घटत रहीम पद, कितौ करो बढि काम ।
तीन पैग वसुधा करो, तऊ बावनै नाम ॥

Begging diminishes one, Rahim, however great the deed;
Crossed the cosmos in three strides, yet known as the dwarf in need!

This is a well-known Puranic episode that Rahim refers to in at least three dohas to impart related but different lessons. Following the traditions of Hindi poetry, he employed images and incidents from the Hindu religious texts to write poetry, which need not necessarily hold personal meaning for him. This is also true for other metaphors that Rahim uses. An object may be used as a positive metaphor in one doha whereas in another it may acquire a negative value. For instance, in the following doha, the pawn is celebrated for its straightforwardness:

फरजी साह न है सके, गति टेढी तासीर।
रहिमन सीधे चालसों, प्यादो होत वजीर॥

The queen cannot become king, by nature it's crooked;
Pawns get to be queen, Rahim, by moving straight ahead.

However, in this instance, the same pawn is deemed an upstart:

जो रहीम ओछो बढ़ै, तौ अति ही इतराय ।
प्यादा सों फरजी भयो, टेढ़ो टेढ़ो जाय ॥

Rahim, as lowly men advance, they put on new airs;
When a pawn turns into queen, it only crosswise stirs.

Rahim can hardly be labelled a hypocrite for using the same metaphor in different ways in two dohas. He was, after all, writing poetry!

He expresses a wide range of emotions—including sorrow, love, wit and humour—through felicitous figures of speech reflecting his understanding of the world. Therefore, his exploration of a range of emotions, from the longings of love to the pitfalls of pride, from the relief of release from desire to the sanity imparted by humility is deep yet delicate. Harish Trivedi puts it most aptly: 'There is hardly any other writer in Hindi literature who lived such a tumultuous life at such a high level and also wrote such heart-touching poetry' (Trivedi 2019a, 31).

Not only did Rahim write on a variety of themes, he also explored several themes from different standpoints. Here, a brief excursion into Rahim's dohas on love may prove worthwhile. We find the poet writing often on love in its various aspects that go beyond the perimeters of Riti poetry and Shringar rasa: romantic love, unrequited love, the heartache of separated lovers, love in friendship, and so on. The romantic in Rahim is devastated by the stunning eyes of beautiful women, which feature in several of his dohas. In this case, they may prove to be fatal:

रहिमन तीर की चोट ते, चोट परे बचि जाय ।
नैन बान की चोट ते, चोट परे मरि जाय ॥

Rahim, if struck by arrows you may yet survive,
But you're finished if you are pierced by striking eyes.

Often, Rahim reminds us of the hazardous nature of the path of love and the courage required to negotiate it:

रहिमन मैन-तुरंग चढ़ि, चलिबो पावक माँहि।
प्रेम-पन्थ ऐसो कठिन सबसों निबहत नाँहि ॥

Rahim, astride a horse of wax, race through a field of fire:
The path of love is as trying — everyone can't aspire.

Perhaps recalling Omar Khayyam's famous quatrain, here he pictures the completeness and self-sufficiency of love:

कहा करौं बैकुंठ लै, कल्प बृच्छ की छाँह ।
रहिमन ढाक सुहावनो, जो गल पीतम बाँह ॥

What will I do with heaven, the shade of the Wishing Tree?
Rahiman, drums sound sweet with my lover's arms around me.

Rahim succinctly encompasses the force of unquenchable passion that fires love in the following doha:

जे सुलगे ते बुझि गए, बुझे तो सुलगे नाहिं ।
रहिमन दाहे प्रेम के, बुझि बुझि के सुलगाहिं ॥

Whatever smoulders dies out, what's doused won't burn again;
Rahim says, those charred by love blaze, again and again.

The tussle between the beloved's gloom of separation and the firefly-like shimmer of hope is caught here:

बिरह रूप घन तम भयो, अवधि आस उद्योत ।
ज्यों रहीम भादों निसा, चमकि जात खद्योत ॥

In the gloom of separation hope shines a tiny light,
As glimmering fireflies, Rahim, illume a monsoon night.

Rahim explores not only the facets of romantic love but other kinds of love too, such as that which flourishes between friends or love that strengthens other social relationships, which are more than transactional:

यह न रहीम सराहिए, लेन देन की प्रीति ।
प्रानन बाजी राखिए, हार होय कै जीति ॥

Says Rahim, do not praise love founded on give and take;
You may win or you may lose, but put your life at stake.

And the poet warns us about the danger of treating relationships casually and breaking off with friends or loved ones thoughtlessly:

रहिमन धागा प्रेम का, मत तोड़ो चटकाय ।
टूटे से फिर ना मिले, मिले गाँठ परि जाय ॥

Rahiman, mind the thread of love do not hastily sever;
Once severed it will not join, save with a knot forever.

Finally, Rahim's gratitude, love for God and complete surrender to Him is expressed thus:

जेहि रहीम तन-मन लियो, कियो हिए बिच भौन ।
तासों दुख सुख कहन की, रही बात अब कौन ॥

Rahim, He has my body and mind, in my heart resides;
Now what is left to tell Him of my sorrows and delights?

The above dohas elicit Rahim's insight and fine sensitivity to different kinds of human relationships. Through his poetry, the poet explores the changing yet changeless nature of love, and the role it plays in forming and holding different kinds of bonds among humans, thus revealing the many-dimensional resplendence of love. In the process, his poetry travels beyond the borders of Riti poetry.

Niti & Sound Sense

As we have seen above, Rahim's dohas address numerous facets of the human condition, yet his dohas have come to be known for conveying lessons in Niti, or principles of behaviour or morality. It may not be far-fetched to claim that many generations of children have been introduced to Rahim through his Niti dohas via Hindi textbooks in school. If a wider variety of his dohas had been prescribed in the textbooks, perhaps this unidimensional perception of Rahim would have been much less prevalent and the children's interest in Rahim more durable. Therefore, we need to keep in mind that 'although Rahim wrote dohas of niti, he did not write dohas only of niti' (Pandey 2019, 54).

Niti refers to forms of behaviour, norms of interaction and principles of action, whether in relatively small groups, in society or in the political and economic spheres. A glance at the dohas grouped under different themes in this book reveals an emphasis on lessons learnt from nature, society, experience, stories or the gods. Though oft mistaken for it, 'niti' need not necessarily be founded on morality. It is true that many of the dohas convey moral messages; yet, it is also true that a larger number espouse norms or principles of behaviour that may not always be acceptable by ethical standards drawn from religious texts or ethical codes. Based on his personal experiences and his observation and understanding of the lives of those around him, both in the rarified atmosphere of the court as well as in the crowded bustle of neighbourhoods and marketplaces, Rahim offers through his dohas principles to guide various aspects of life—virtue, wisdom and worldliness. This is based on good sense, acquired through long, varied and often intense extremes of experience, which shines through in most of his dohas.

Rahim was both a man of the world and a poet. His long experience through the thick and thin of life left him without any illusions about what matters in the 'real world'. No wonder he writes:

अब रहीम मुश्किल पड़ी, गाढ़े दोऊ काम ।
साँचे से तो जग नहीं, झूठे मिलैं न राम ॥

Now, Rahim, you're in trouble: both choices are hard;
Truth does not yield this world and lies don't win you God.

Rahim presents a fundamental dilemma: everyone in this world has two basic choices, between truth and untruth. Truth leads to God while untruth earns success in the material world. Rahim implies that we may choose between material success or spiritual fulfilment, not both; indeed a hard choice.

Clearly, for Abdur Rahim, behaviour that is acceptable to a worldly person would not measure up to the yardstick of the pious. But even such persons may need to adopt certain 'working strategies', if not 'principles', that may help clear their path to success. Therefore, Rahim says:

रहिमन जो रहिबो चहै, कहै वाहि के दाँव।
जो बासर को निस कहै, तौ कचपची दिखाव॥

Rahim, if you'd be in with them, agree with what they say;
If they declare that day is night, point out the Milky Way.

Not only do Rahim's dohas point out the right forms of behaviour, they also indicate what constitutes injudicious conduct that should be shunned, as in:

रोल बिगाड़े राज नै, मोल बिगाड़े माल॥
सनै सनै सरदार की, चुगल बिगाड़े चाल॥

Kings spoil the rule of law while traders ruin trade;
And, bit by bit, backbiting blights the leader's ways.

We find Rahim's poetry marked by the dominance of sound sense over emotions, of mind over heart. Although his verse reflects poetic sensibility in subjects where feelings are in focus, Rahim often gives precedence to the message. For instance, when he dwells upon the loneliness of sorrow, he notes:

रहिमन निज मन की विथा, मन ही राखो गोय ।
सुनि अठिलैहैं लोग सब, बाँटि न लैहैं कोय ॥

Rahim warns, lock up your grief within your heart. Beware!
If folks find out they'll just sneer, not one of them will share.

Perhaps born of the poet's personal experience, without dwelling upon a particular sorrow and its cause, the couplet voices a clear message: don't share your grief with others, because people are more likely to make fun of it than sympathise.

Rahim prescribes lessons for individual well-being as well as for the individual in society. Conscious of the vast disparities of wealth and power in the world around him, he postulates that, to survive in an unequal society, it may be necessary to come to terms with harsh realities:

कैसे निबहैं निबल जन, करि सबलन सों गैर ।
रहिमन बसि सागर बिषे, करत मगर सों वैर ॥

How can weak folk get by if they turn mighty
men hostile?
Those who live in water, Rahim, daren't cross
the crocodile.

Good sense informs Rahim's dohas. For instance, in the section 'On Discernment', as a poet of good sense, Rahim makes connections between disparate objects by pointing out a common uniting characteristic:

खैर, खून, खाँसी, खुसी, बैर, प्रीति, मदपान ।
रहिमन दाबे न दबैं, जानत सकल जहान ॥

Catechu, murder, cough, joy, ill will, love, drunkenness—
Rahim, the whole world comes to know, no one can
suppress.

Always perceptive, Rahim's wit is unsparing of affectation:

करत निपुनई गुन बिना, रहिमन निपुन हजूर।
मानहु टेरत बिटप चढ़ि, मोहि समान को कूर॥

To brag without talent, Rahim, before an able chief,
Is like shouting from a treetop, 'Is there a dunce like me?'

No sequence has been found assigned to Rahim's dohas or his other poetry, especially since 'we have little by way of historical markers in them of references to datable events or persons' (Raghavan 2017, 136). Therefore, most compilers have arranged the dohas alphabetically. There are several dohas that do not carry the poet's signature, 'Rahiman' or 'Rahim'. Yajnik considers these suspect. Besides, there are certain dohas that do carry Rahim's signature (1928,16), which he believes are by other poets.

As widely noted, there is little doubt that Rahim's dohas reflect the many ups and downs in his long life and career. It is even possible to recognise the circumstances that prompted the poet to write certain dohas. However, it does not appear possible to identify the specific episodes or even phases during which he wrote them. Over and over in his long life, Rahim found himself facing similar circumstances and turbulence. For instance, let us examine the subject of 'fate' in Rahim's dohas—a theme more recurrent than others, conceivably because it affected him more. He wrote at least six dohas on fate (see section 'On Fate'), the central message of each being the complete dominance and inexorability of destiny:

ज्यों नाचत कठपूतरी, करम नचावत गात ।
अपने हाथ रहीम ज्यों, नहीं आपुने हाथ ॥

We are like prancing puppets, Fate makes us all dance;
Just as our own hands, Rahim, are not in our hands.

To further emphasise the point, in several dohas, Rahim alludes to the fate of the leading characters of the Mahabharata and Ramayana, as in:

महि नभ सर पंजर कियो, रहिमन बल अवसेष ।
सो अर्जुन बैराट घर, रहे नारि के भेष ॥

Great Arjuna with arrows, Rahim, covered the earth and sky;
That Arjuna lived in Virat's house perforce in woman's guise.

As is apparent, neither of these dohas holds the minutest of clues about the phase of misfortune during which they were written. This is true of other dohas that too appear to have been drawn from deeply personal episodes. For instance, in this doha:

होत कृपा जो बड़ेन की, सो कदाचि घटि जाय ॥
तौ रहीम मरिबो भलो, यह दुःख सहो न जाय ॥

If of elders' blessings one is suddenly bereft,
It's better to die, Rahim, this grief one can't accept.

Rahim might have been grieving the death of Akbar, yet nothing in the doha confirms that this is indeed the case.

Mayashankar Yajnik is right in noting how remarkable it is that, despite spending almost his entire life on the battlefield, Rahim wrote no poems in veer rasa (the heroic aesthetic), and that, though his experiences are reflected in the dohas, no specific fact or incident is mentioned (Yajnik 1928, 17). It is as if Rahiman ensured that nothing in his poetry could be misconstrued by the Khan-i-Khanan's rivals and antagonists in court who were always eager to conspire against him.

The Structure

This book has been organised with the objective of making its contents easily accessible to the reader. A list of Source Texts follows this introduction so that readers who wish to pursue their interest in Rahim may consult the anthologies of his works. A bibliography of the works consulted is included at the end of the book. The Table of Contents tells the reader that the dohas are grouped in thirty thematic sections, presented alphabetically. One may contend that that is too many sections, but the aim is to enable readers to indulge their mood and curiosity and easily identify dohas on a topic that may be on their mind or look up dohas on a theme that strikes their fancy. A bibliography follows the thematic sections. To facilitate easy location of any doha in the book, an index of the first half of first lines in both Hindi (Devanagari) and English has also been provided at the end of the book. Abdur Rahim was a man of eclectic interests, and a poet who drew upon both his scholarship and his experiences in his writings and poetry. It is also hoped that the clustering of Rahim's dohas into these themes might facilitate ready access to the invaluable insights of a complex, empathetic and thoughtful man who led a highly eventful life.

Each page carries a doha in the original (with its source), followed by a translation into the English and a brief elucidation. Thus, bilingual readers may savour the original and compare it with the translation and the explanation. The first anthology of Rahim's work that I came upon, and to which I am indebted for an extensive introduction to the poet, was Deshraj Singh Bhati's *Rahim Granthavali* (2011). This was followed by Vidyaniwas Mishra and Govind Rajneesh's compilation of the same name (2005). I have included two dohas from Mayashankar Yajnik's *Rahim Ratnavali*. Though I have used Mishra–Rajneesh as the principal text, all three of these books are Source Books for this work.

When I began working on the explanations, it was evident that there are several dohas that hardly need any. But there are also a large number that draw upon stories from the Ramayana and Mahabharata or use illustrations from the Puranas that some readers would be unfamiliar with. The focus is on explicating the allusions in the dohas that are usually set in a larger context. The more straightforward dohas, whose meaning is self-evident, have not been elaborated further. Therefore, for some dohas the explanation is but a sentence long, while for quite a few others, they run on for half a page or more.

In conclusion, I must clarify two points: one, that the responsibility of the interpretation of the dohas, along with translating them, is entirely mine; two, in selecting the dohas presented in this volume, I have followed only my preferences. Almost half of Rahim's dohas find place here, but it would be foolish to say that the dohas in this selection sparkle more than those not included here. Each of them is a finely cut and polished gem. In deference to Rahim's advice, I read them again and again, for as he says:

रूप, कथा, पद, चारु पट, कंचन, दोहा, लाल।
ज्यों-ज्यों निरखत सूक्ष्म गति, मोल रहीम बिसाल॥

Beauty, parable, verse, fine clothes, rubies, couplets and gold—
As you slowly examine each, its worth grows manifold.

Source Texts

Bhati (followed by doha no. and page no.): Deshraj Singh (ed.). *Rahim Granthavali*. New Delhi: Naman Prakashan, 2011.

M&R (followed by doha no. and page no.): Mishra, Vidyaniwas and Rajneesh, Govind (eds). *Rahim Granthavali*. New Delhi: Zenith Publishers, 2005.

MSY (followed by doha no. and page no): Yajnik, Mayashankar (ed). *Rahim Ratnavali*. Kashi: Sahitya Seva Sadan, 1928.

*

Note: The motifs on the section-opening pages are based on the medallions engraved on the arches in the mausoleum of Abdur Rahim Khan-i-Khanan on Mathura Road, Delhi.

On Doha

दीरघ दोहा अरथ के, आखर थोरे आहिं।
ज्यों रहीम नट कुंडली, सिमटी कूदि चढ़ि जाहिं॥

M&R: 105: 79

Couplets comprise a few letters but hold abundant sense;
As the crouching acrobat, Rahim, springs atop the fence.

Explaining the nature of the doha, Rahim states that in a few words the doha packs a great deal of meaning. The force of a doha comes as a bit of a surprise, just like the performance of a small acrobat who gathers herself and springs up onto a high fence or line. Although short of stature, acrobats perform feats disproportionately large, as the doha of two lines conveys a message of great moment.

The reference here is to the groups of wandering acrobats that used to frequent the countryside or towns in India, putting up shows at street corners.

On Affectation/ False Pride

करत निपुनई गुन बिना, रहिमन निपुन हजूर।
मानहु टेरत बिटप चढ़ि, मोहि समान को कूर॥

M&R: 28: 71

To brag without talent, Rahim, in front of an able chief,
Is like shouting from a treetop, 'Is there a dunce like me?'

If we wish to impress our superiors in front of others, we must have talent, ability or achievement that speaks for us. Without this, Rahim warns us, such attempts may merely publicise our foolishness. Therefore, desist from boasting.

थोथे बादल क्वाँर के, ज्यों रहीम घहरात ॥
धनी पुरुष निर्धन भये, करै पाछिली बात ॥

M&R: 100: 79

Rahim says, in the month of Kwar, hollow clouds whirl and roar,
Like penniless men, who once were rich, brag of what's no more.

Kwar is the month in the Hindu calendar that marks the transition between the rainy season and winter. Normally, it occupies the second half of September and the first half of October and is characterised by the drying of the wet earth. The retreating monsoon clouds bear little moisture, but they do thunder menacingly from time to time. They bring to Rahim's mind once-wealthy men who crow about their 'good days' from the past. Now, such people can do little more than recall their lost grandeur.

On Beautiful Eyes

जो रहिम जग मारियो, नैन बान की चोट।
भगत भगत कोउ बचि गये, चरन कमल कि ओट॥

M&R: 86: 77

If the world is assailed, Rahim, by darts from lovely eyes,
At His lotus feet a fleeing devotee may survive.

In his dohas Rahim often catches moments that seize the essence of the context and the action framed in it. The above doha is a warning to the romantically inclined: the adventurous are likely to be attacked by sharp glances shot at them by beautiful eyes; only devotees of the Lord who seek refuge in Him may survive the arrows from the death-dealing eyes of the beloved. In other words, only unwavering love of God is stronger than devastating earthly love.

प्रीतम छबि नैनन बसी, पर छबि कहाँ समाय ।
भरी सराय रहीम लखि, पथिक आप फिर जाय ॥

M&R: 129: 82

The lover's image fills the eye, where can another stay?
Finding the inn crowded, Rahim, travellers turn away.

The above doha may echo someone's (perhaps even the poet's own) disappointment in unrequited love. Rahim tries to console the lover by using the simile of an inn; if a traveller approaches an inn that is full, he shall be turned away. Similarly, if the eyes of the beloved can see only her loved one, how can other aspirants' love be reciprocated?

रहिमन तीर की चोट ते, चोट परे बचि जाय ।
नैन बान की चोट ते, चोट परे मरि जाय ॥

M&R: 207: 90

Rahim, if struck by arrows you may yet survive,
But you're finished if you are pierced by striking eyes.

The poet in a romantic mood warns us about the dangers of love. One may survive if hit by an arrow. However, if one falls for the beautiful eyes of a woman, there is no chance of recovery.

रहिमन सो न कछू गनै, जासों लागे नैन ।
सहि के सोच बेसाहियो, गयो हाथ को चैन ॥

M&R: 253: 95

Rahim, I mean nothing to the one I've lost my heart;
It's true, love is buying pain and seeing peace depart.

Rahim laments that his beloved thinks nothing of him, that in her eyes he has no worth. Like other lovers before him, he discovers that by falling in love he has lost his peace of mind without gaining anything in return.

On Unsound Beginnings

रहिमन खोटी आदि की, सो परिनाम लखाय।
जैसे दीपक तम भखै, कज्जल वमन कराय॥

M&R: 192: 89

A poor beginning, Rahim, presages the output;
A lamp that devours darkness is sure to vomit soot.

In this doha Rahim states that anything that has a flawed beginning is likely to have unsatisfactory results. In this regard, he points at the oil lamp lit at even-fall. By lighting up the area, the lamp swallows the darkness around it, but it also emits smoke and soot. Rahim is here restating an idea that is often found in dohas—as you sow, so you reap.

बिगरी बात बने नहीं, लाख करो किन कोय ।
रहिमन फाटे दूध को, मथे न माखन होय ॥

M&R: 140: 83

Botched affairs do not mend, though you may try a million tricks;
Rahiman, you can't make butter by churning curdled milk.

Rahim is of the view that once a venture has gone wrong, it cannot be set straight. He reminds us of the futility of trying to make butter from curdled milk. It is best, therefore, to cut one's losses early and move on to something else.

रहिमन बिगरी आदि की, बनै न खरचे दाम ।
हरि बाढ़े आकाश लौं, तउ बावनै नाम ॥

M&R: 227: 92

Spending a fortune, says Rahim, can't mend what's ill-begun;
Though Hari soared up to the sky, He's Dwarf to everyone.

Rahim tells us that any enterprise that is flawed or initiated for the wrong reasons is bound to go wrong.

Egged on by the disgruntled suras, Lord Vishnu approached Bali in the guise of a poor dwarf brahmin and begged him to grant him only as much land as he might cover in three strides. Although aware of the true identity of the brahmin, Bali agreed, whereupon, abandoning the guise of a dwarf, Vishnu assumed a gigantic stature; in his first stride he covered the heavens, in the second he covered the earth and, since nothing else remained, Bali offered his own head that Vishnu claimed by placing his foot upon it. Thereafter, Bali was banished to the netherworld.

Although Vishnu vanquished Bali, he stood vanquished in the eyes of the world, forever to be called *Baman*, the Dwarf!

On Begging

माँगे घटत रहीम पद, कितौ करौ बढि काम ।
तीन पैग बसुधा करो, तउ बावनै नाम ॥

M&R: 155: 85

Begging diminishes one, Rahim, however great the deed;
Crossed the cosmos in three strides, yet known as the dwarf in need!

Rahim refers in this couplet to the story of Lord Vishnu tricking the generous King Bali out of his kingdom, as described earlier, on p. 14–15.

Through the story, he wishes to highlight that anyone who goes begging loses respect for ever.

रहिमन वे नर मर चुके, जे कहुँ माँगन जाहिं ।
उनते पहिले वे मुए, जिन मुख निकसत नाहिं ॥

M&R: 250: 95

The man who goes out begging is long dead, Rahim,
And yet, before him died they who said 'No' to him.

Rahim, a man renowned for unrestrained charity, says that persons who go around begging are as good as dead because they have already lost their sense of self-respect, and without self-respect their identity is lost. But those who heartlessly denied him help can be said to have died even earlier, having lost their humanity.

On Bravery

लोहे की न लोहार का, रहिमन कही विचार।
जो हनि मारै सीस में, ताही की तलवार॥

M&R: 262: 96

Neither the blacksmith's nor of iron, musing says Rahim,
He who directly strikes the head, the sword belongs to him.

The above doha forces one to think about the nature of our relationship with things around us, especially objects of utility—an implement, a piece of equipment or a weapon. Using the example of a sword, Rahim raises questions about the reason for its existence, and its ownership. What is a sword? To whom does it belong? What is significant—the iron it is made of or the person who made it, the blacksmith? Rahim asserts that the sword belongs to the person who can best use it to strike the enemy's head, to kill him. Which is to say that an instrument belongs in the hands of the person who can use it most effectively.

साधु सराहै साधुता, जती जोखिता जान।
रहिमन साँचै सूर को, बैरी करै बखान॥

M&R: 279: 98

Pious folk applaud piety, yogis unworldly ways;
Rahiman, on the truly brave enemies shower praise.

In general, people value qualities in others that they recognise in themselves. For instance, good people admire those who are ethical while yogis respect those who reject the material and embrace the spiritual. However, the truly valorous warrior is admired and lauded even by his foes and rivals.

On Charity/Giving

तब ही लौ जीबो भलो, दीबो होय न धीम।
जग में रहिबो कुचित गति, उचित न होय रहीम॥

M&R: 95: 78

Life is worth living only for as long as one can give;
Being in a shrunk state, Rahim, is not the way to live.

Abdur Rahim Khan-i-Khanan was widely known for his generosity to the needy and the deserving. Giving alms to the poor or rewards to poets, artists and soldiers was almost a habit with him. This doha appears to have been written during difficult times when he was not in a position to follow through on his instinct for generosity; it expresses his conviction that life is worth living only so long as one is in a position to give to others, help others.

तरुवर फल नहीं खात हैं, सरवर पियहिं न पान।
कहि रहीम पर काज हित, संपति सँचहि सुजान॥

M&R: 96: 78

Trees never savour their fruit, lakes don't drink their water;
The wise amass wealth, Rahim, but for the use of others.

Not only was Rahim generous with his wealth, helping everyone who sought his assistance, he also exhorted others to help the less fortunate. In this couplet he asks us to learn charity from nature. Just as trees do not partake of the fruits they bear nor do lakes drink their own water, wise people should save money to spend on those in need of aid.

तासों ही कछु पाइए, कीजै जाकी आस।
रीते सरवर पर गये, कैसे बुझै पियास॥

M&R: 97: 78

You may receive only from those you trust will provide;
At a lake that has gone dry, can thirst be satisfied?

Using the metaphor of a dried-up lake, Rahim states that there is little point in seeking help from those who either have nothing to give or are not inclined to help others. One should seek help only from those one may rely upon. In sum, do not waste effort and time in seeking help from one and all.

वे रहीम नर धन्य हैं, पर उपकारी अंग।
बाँटनवारे को लगे, ज्यों मेहंदी को रंग ॥

M&R: 267: 97

Rahim, such folks are blessed who come to others' aid:
Hands that give out henna also take on its shade.

Compassionate and generous persons who practice charity are truly fortunate. Charitable folk receive by giving, just as the person who beautifies the hands and feet of others by making patterns with henna finds her own hands dyed by it.

हित रहीम इतऊ करै, जाकी जिती बिसात ।
नहिं यह रहै न वह रहै, रहै कहन को बात ॥

M&R: 288: 99

Help others, Rahim observes, with what you can afford;
Neither one nor the other lasts, only the record.

Rahim, himself a large-hearted man, advises that one should not be close-fisted when lending a hand to someone in need. Instead, one should give as much as one can. Neither the giver nor the receiver will live for ever, but the deed will stay on in people's memory.

रहिमन पर उपकार के, करत न यारी बीच ।
मांस दियो शिवि भूप ने, दीन्हों हाड़ दधीच ॥

M&R: 35: 72

Rahim says, friendship can't stand between you
and charity:
King Shibi gave over his flesh and his bones
gave Dadhichi.

Rahim emphasises the importance of selfless charity by recalling the legends of King Shibi and the sage Dadhichi.

According to the Jatakas, King Shibi was sitting in his court when a dove pursued by a falcon flew in and took shelter in his lap. The falcon demanded of the king that since the dove was his food, it should be handed over to him. King Shibi, caught between his duty as king to protect anyone who sought shelter and the right of another to partake of its food, without hesitation cut off a portion of his own flesh and gave it to the falcon.

The Bhagwata Purana tells us that defeated by Vrita, Prajapati's son, Indra and the suras were in a quandary. They went to Lord Vishnu, who told them that Vrita could be killed with a weapon fashioned from the bones of Sage Dadhichi. Indra approached Dadhichi and sought his help in defeating Vrita, who posed a threat to all suras. Dadhichi agreed to donate his bones and gave up his breath. Indra made Vajra, the weapon, with Dadhichi's bones and finally destroyed Vrita.

Thus, Rahim points out that giving may require you to abandon love of all things, including the self.

On Company

कहु रहीम कैसे निभै, बेर केर को संग ।
वे डोलत रस आपने, उनके फाटत अंग ॥

M&R: 35: 72

Rahim, how can thorny ber and banana shrubs be friends?
Plump with juice they swing about while their limbs are torn to shreds!

Ber, jujube berries, grow on branches covered with nettles. Any other tree or shrub near it can only suffer from its closeness, especially if it has soft, large leaves like the banana plant, which can tear on contact with the thorns. Rahim indicates that a relationship between crude and gentle folk is inevitably fraught; the two cannot be friends.

बसि कुसंग चाहत कुसल, यह रहीम जिय सोस ।
महिमा घटी समुद की, रावन बस्यो परोस ॥

M&R: 138: 83

If you keep vile company, Rahim, can you hope to thrive?
The ocean lost its greatness since Ravana lived nearby.

Keeping the company of wicked persons or residing in the neighbourhood of the villainous brings one into disrepute. For the world may also choose to treat you summarily and without respect. Rahim recalls that even the mighty ocean was denied respect because it was close to Ravana's kingdom. Lord Rama, by building a bridge of floating stones across the ocean to Lanka, demonstrated to the world that it was not as great or unassailable as was once believed.

रहिमन नीचन संग बसि, लगत कलंक न काहि ।
दूध कलारी कर गहे, मद समुझै सब ताहि ॥

M&R: 216: 91

Rahim, if you live with lowly folk, why won't taint adhere?
The brewer holds a mug of milk, yet all believe it's beer!

Rahim tells us that we are often identified by the company we keep. The habits, character and mannerisms of our friends are often reflected in us as well. Little wonder, then, that even when a brewer sips milk from a mug, he is mistaken for a drunkard.

On Desire/Maya

भार झोंकि के भार में, रहिमन उतरे पार ।
पै बूड़े मझधार में, जिनके सिर पर भार ॥

M&R: 144: 84

Rahim torched his burden and crossed to the far side;
Those who come with head heaped high sink
midstream betide.

The above doha resembles, and perhaps draws from, the Bhakti poetry of the age.[1] Rahim says that he is assured of salvation, having rid himself of his burdens. It is not clear whether Rahim's burdens are his 'sins', which he has burnt in the fire of repentance, or worldly desires, which he

1 See, for instance:

Kabir, the boat is frail, its rowers weak and lank.
The lightest lightly swam across, those laden heavy sank.

The Vision of Wisdom, Kabir: Selected Sakhis. New Delhi, Rupa Publications, 2020. p.155.

has scorched with the flames of Bhakti—devotion. However, he makes it clear that sinners or those embroiled in earthly desires (and the two may mean the same here) cannot reach God. Those who carry the head-load of their sins/desires are sure to sink in the worldly ocean well before they reach their destination—salvation.

बहु रहीम केतिक रही, केतिक गई बिहाय।
माया ममता मोह परि, अंत चले पछिताय॥

Bhati: 33: 102

Rahim, so much is left of life although so much is past,
Caught in greed, love and desire, with regret we leave at last.

Commenting on the plight of humans, Rahim says that despite the riches we may have enjoyed, we are seldom satisfied with what we have. It often turns out that towards the end of life, we look back and feel trammelled by the love of things and people, realising that life has been frittered away in the pursuit of desire. Then, only regret remains.

चाह गई चिंता मिटी, मनुआ बेपरवाह ।
जिनको कछू न चाहिए, वे साहन के साह ॥

M&R: 56: 74

If desires go, cares go, the mind is free of all things.
Those who yearn for nothing are truly the king of kings.

Rahim identifies desire as the cause of most worries. It is because people constantly want more that they are never at peace. Therefore, he says, if one wishes to be truly free of unhappiness, one must rid oneself of desire. Thus, those who do not want anything and can rule over their desire are more powerful than kings.

करम-हीन रहिमन लखो, धँसो बड़े घर चोर।
चिन्तत ही बड़ लाभ के, जागत ह्वै गो भोर॥

M&R: 29: 71

Behold the luckless thief, Rahim, break into a rich home;
Dreaming of stupendous gain, he tarries there till it's dawn.

Rahim illustrates the saying that the greed of knaves often proves to be their undoing with the example of a thief who enters a prosperous house. Finding it full of riches, the greedy man begins to think about how wealthy he is about to become and how he is going to enjoy the wealth. While he is engaged in these delightful contemplations, night turns into morning and he is caught by the waking household.

रहिमन अपने पेट सौ, बहुत कह्यो समुझाय।
जो तू अन खाये रहे, तोसों को अनखाये॥

M&R: 177: 87

Rahim, I tell my stomach, and try hard to explain:
If you go without food, why would anyone complain?

Rahim says that he has tried to convince his stomach that if only it could go without food, there would be no cause for grief. In a roundabout way, the poet is asking us to recognise that our stomach, which signifies desire, is the main cause of our sufferings.

On Discernment

दोनों रहिमन एक से, जौ लौं बोलत नाहिं ।
जान परत हैं काक पिक, ऋतु बसंत के माँहिं ॥

M&R: 110: 80

Rahim, both appear the same as long as they hold their tongue;
One can tell crow from cuckoo when the season turns to spring.

As long as neither the crow nor the cuckoo (koyal) makes a sound, it may not be possible to tell the birds apart. However, with the advent of spring and balmy weather, when the birds begin to sing, the difference between the two becomes all too obvious. Through this couplet Rahim indicates that appearances are often deceptive; one must wait for people to act, or at least speak, to understand their true nature.

ससि की सीतल चाँदनी, सुंदर सबहिं सुहाय।
लगे चोर चित में लटी, घटि रहीम मन आय॥

M&R: 283: 98

Everyone regards as pleasing the cool moonlight serene;
Save for the thief who is happy when it is gone, Rahim.

Using the example of moonlight, Rahim makes a simple point: our perception of what is good or bad is often determined by our requirements and priorities. Almost everyone finds moonlight to be calming and pleasing, yet it vexes those whose intentions may be dubious—in this instance, thieves. In other words, that which is good for society offends the anti-social.

पावस देखि रहीम मन, कोइल साधे मौन ।
अब दादुर वक्ता भए, हमको पूछत कौन ॥

M&R: 126: 82

Spying dark clouds, Rahim, the koyal holds its tongue;
Frogs have turned orators, who cares now for my song?

The koyal, or cuckoo, is known for its melodious call during the summer months. However, as the monsoon clouds approach, the koyal stops singing; once the rains begin, only the croaking of frogs is heard. Referring to this seasonal occurrence, Rahim indicates that difficult times are approaching and it may be best for him to keep quiet and lie low, for it is a time when others, though harsh-tongued, are more likely to be heard.

भूप गनत लघु गुनिन को, गुनी गुनत लघु भुप ।
रहिमन गिर ते भूमिलौं, लखौ तौ एकै रुप ॥

M&R: 148: 84

The king deems artists to be low, to them he is small;
Rahim from peaks to the plains, sees one visage in all.

Preoccupied by our own standards, we look down upon others. For instance, kings/rulers, consider artists, rich in talent and skills, as not of much worth. They, in turn, look down upon those wielding power as unworthy of respect. Yet, says Rahim, from the mountains to the plains, one can see only one visage in all creatures—that of the creator. Thus, in one sweeping gesture Rahim negates all manifestations of ego and reminds us that all of us have the same maker.

मन से कहाँ रहीम प्रभु, दृग सो कहाँ दिवान ।
देखि दृगन जो आदरै, मन तेहि हाथ बिकान ॥

M&R: 151: 84

Where is a king like the mind, a premier like the eye?
That which the eye finds worthy, the mind is sure to buy.

Although the mind reigns supreme in the human body, Rahim says that it is guided principally by the eyes. For the eye is able to distinguish and estimate that which is most valuable. Hence, while calling the mind the sovereign, Rahim assigns the eye the position of prime minister, or the chief arbiter of good and evil.

रहिमन तीन प्रकार ते, हित अनहित पहिचानि ।
पर बस परे, परोस बस, परे मामिला जानि ॥

M&R: 206: 90

Rahim, there are three ways to know who is good
and who evil:
While in their power, living nearby or in a fight legal.

How can we know the true nature of people around us—whether they are good or evil? According to Rahim, the three kinds of circumstances in which we may do so are: when we are in their control; if they are our neighbours; and, if we enter into a litigation with them. In these three situations, we would be impacted directly by their actions and behaviour and, therefore, able to best assess their true nature.

रहिमन जगत बड़ाई की, कूकुर की पहिचानि।
प्रीति करै मुख चाटई, बैर करे तन हानि॥

M&R: 197: 89

Flatterers of this world, Rahim, to dogs one may equate;
When fond of you they lick your face, but bite you if they hate.

To Rahim, an acute observer and student of human character, sycophants were always suspect. Through his poetry he often condemns flattery and flatterers. In this doha he asks us to beware of flatterers; they are like dogs who, when they love you, will fawn over you and lick your face, but if repulsed, may bite you at the first opportunity. One might add, though, that here Rahim is being unkind to dogs!

खैर, खून, खाँसी, खुसी, बैर, प्रीति, मदपान ।
रहिमन दाबे न दबैं, जानत सकल जहान ॥

M&R: 49: 74

Catechu, murder, cough, joy, ill will, love, drunkenness—
Rahim, the whole world comes to know, no one
can suppress.

Try as one might, there are some things that cannot be hidden from the world. Those who chew paan cannot conceal the red colour of betel juice—caused chiefly by the ingredient catechu and the betel leaf—on their lips and teeth; spilt blood, that is, in a clash or a murder cannot be hidden (although 'खून' or 'blood' here may also refer to lineage, whether 'high' or 'low'); a cough will be heard; happiness shows on one's face; hatred and love will find expression in words and/or deeds; and drunkenness is evident in one's behaviour.

सबको सब कोऊ करै, कै सलाम कै राम।
हित रहीम तब जानिए, जब कछु अटकै काम ॥

M&R: 269: 97

Everyone offers greetings, some say 'Salaam', some 'Ram'.
You'll discern your friends, Rahim, when you are in a jam.

Under normal circumstances, everyone is polite and pleasant to others. However, civility alone does not make for friendship. Rahim points out that one discovers one's well-wishers in circumstances beyond the formalities of everyday interaction. Only those who lend a hand in demanding times can be said to be friends.

On Ego

कागद को सो पूतरा, सहजहि में घुलि जाय ।
रहिमन यह अचरज लखो, सोऊ खैंचत बाय ॥

M&R: 37: 72

This doll made up of paper scraps, which easily dissolves—
Rahim, isn't it marvellous that it too swells up with pride?

Remarking on the irony of human existence, Rahim contrasts the fragility of the physical frame with the robustness of the ego. Although we are as flimsily built as dolls made of scraps of paper and rags that a mere splash of water can ruin, we think no end of ourselves, and are forever self-importantly broadcasting our achievements.

रहिमन मनहिं लगाइ के, देखि लेहु किन कोय ।
नर को बस करिबो कहा, नारायण बस होय ॥

M&R: 229: 93

Rahim asks, why not reflect and truly search your soul?
What is there for man to do? The Lord is in control.

Addressing those who believe they are the masters of their world, Rahim asks that they carefully deliberate and consider their position in the universe. They would realise then that there is very little in this life that is determined by humans; the world is run by the will of God.

रहिमन गली है साँकरी, दूजो न ठहराहिं।
आपु अहै तो हरि नहीं, हरि तो आपुन नाहिं॥

M&R: 193: 89

Rahim says, the lane is narrow, there is no room to spare.
If I'm there, Hari is not; if Hari is I'm not there.

Ego leaves no room for anyone or anything else. Rahim makes it clear that until one is able to rid oneself of ego, one cannot expect to find God.

On Fate

ज्यों नाचत कठपूतरी, करम नचावत गात ।
अपने हाथ रहीम ज्यों, नहीं आपुने हाथ ॥

M&R: 63: 75

We are like prancing puppets, Fate makes us all dance;
Just as our own hands, Rahim, are not in our hands.

Using yet another simile, Rahim underscores the omnipotence of Fate. He likens people to puppets on invisible strings that Destiny plays with to make them dance. Therefore, says the poet, be it our limbs or our affairs, they are not in our control, though we appear to direct them. Fate is our puppeteer.

जो पुरूषारथ ते कहूँ, संपति मिलत रहीम।
पेट लागि वैराट घर, तपत रसोई भीम ॥

M&R: 78: 76

If but by industry, Rahim, one could earn great riches,
Just to fill his belly would Bhim sweat in Virat's kitchen?

Pointing at the role Destiny plays in a person's life, Rahim says that mere courage, strength and industry do not ensure wealth.

Drawing from the Virata Parva, the fourth book of the Mahabharata, Rahim cites the example of Bhim, the strongest of the five Pandava brothers. During their period of exile, the Pandavas had to spend the last, the thirteenth, year, incognito. Therefore, in disguise they found employment in the palace of King Virat of Matsya kingdom. Bhim, or 'Ballava', became a cook in the royal kitchen under the name and earned his living labouring in front of the stoves.

जो रहीम भावी कतौं, होति आपुने हाथ ।
राम न जाते हरिन संग, सीय न रावन साथ ॥

M&R: 90: 78

Rahim, if we could look ahead and our future control,
Rama would not pursue the deer nor Sita with
Ravana go.

Rahim underscores the importance of Destiny in our lives. Speaking of the impossibility of predicting the future, he reminds us that if what lay before them could have been known in advance, in the Ramayana, neither would Rama have gone in pursuit of the golden hind nor would Sita have stepped beyond the Lakshman Rekha to give Ravana the chance to kidnap her.

निज कर क्रिया रहीम कहि, सिधि भावी के हाथ ।
पाँसे अपने हाथ में, दाँव न अपने हाथ ॥

M&R: 120: 81

Do your duty, says Rahim, the end Future unfolds;
True, the dice is in our hand, but not the way it rolls.

The outcome of all our actions will be known by and by. Rahim reminds us that in the game of life, our role is limited to throwing the dice; we cannot influence the way they fall. Virtually echoing the Gita, Rahim here advises us to do our duty and not focus on the result.

भावी काहू ना दही, भावी दह भगवान ।
भावी ऐसी प्रबल है, कही रहीम यह जान ॥

M&R: 145: 84

No one can destroy Fate. Fate did not spare the Lord.
That's how forceful Fate is—Rahim says, mark my word.

In this couplet Rahim returns to one of his favourite themes: the importance of Fate. He asks us never to underestimate the force of Fate. The poet hints at the example of Lord Rama; even he had to go through the travails of a fourteen-year-long exile from Ayodhya that Fate had in store for him. Thus, Rahim indicates that Fate is more powerful than even the gods.

महि नभ सर पंजर कियो, रहिमन बल अवसेष ।
सो अर्जुन बैराट घर, रहे नारि के भेष ॥

M&R: 154: 85

Great Arjuna with arrows, Rahim, covered the earth and sky;
That Arjuna lived in Virat's house, perforce in woman's guise.

In the above doha Rahim again underlines the importance of Fate and its inevitability. Taking the example of Arjuna, the Pandava prince, he reminds us that such was the prowess of the supreme warrior that during the battle with Indra and the other gods over the Khandava forest, Arjun defeated them by covering the earth and the sky with arrows. However, that same Arjun had to spend a year disguised as a woman in the palace of King Virata of the Matasya kingdom where he taught dance to Princess Uttara.

On Friends & Friendship

आवत काज रहीम कहि, गाढ़े बंधु सनेह ।
जीरन होत न पेड़ ज्यौं, थामै बरै बरेह ॥

M&R: 16: 70

The affection of staunch friends, Rahim, can be of great use;
Just as banyans don't weaken, held up by aerial roots.

Rahim states a truth that has been rediscovered by generations: in old age, it is the companionship of affectionate friends, siblings and relatives that provides one with support. Like the aerial roots of the banyan tree, they hold us up, physically and morally. Therefore, we must value old friends and family.

ए रहीम दर-दर फिरहिं, माँगि मधुकरी खाहिं ।
यारो यारी छोड़िए, वे रहीम अब नाहिं ॥

M&R: 21: 71

Rahim goes from door to door, begging for every meal.
Friends bid goodbye to friendship! This isn't the same Rahim.

While going through a difficult time, Rahim points to his own disempowered condition and warns his friends that they should not expect anything from him. Although known for his large-heartedness, in his present circumstances he has nothing to offer them; indeed, he is himself dependent on others. With this frank declaration of penury, perhaps Rahim also seeks to find out who among his circle of friends will stay by him when he is down and out.

जैसी तुम हमसों करी, करी करो जो तीर।
बाढ़े दिन के मीत हौ, गाढ़े दिन रघुबीर॥

M&R: 75: 76

You've done to me what the herd did to the elephant by the shore.
You're but a fair-weather friend, in trouble God is my succour.

In the above lines Rahim appears to be reproaching a friend who has not stood by him in a time of need. He recalls the story of the elephant whose life was saved by Lord Krishna.

One day, the elephant king and his herd were drinking water at a lake. Suddenly, a monstrous crocodile caught his leg and began to pull him into the depths. The elephant king tried to free himself and called out to the other elephants for help, but they ran away. He then cried aloud to Shri Krishna, seeking his intervention. Krishna appeared and saved his devotee by killing the crocodile. This story finds repeated reference in Rahim's poetry.

Rahim concludes his castigation by calling his friends selfish and asserting that during hard times, one may rely only upon God's help.

धन दारा अरू सुतन सों, लगो रहे नित चित्त ।
नहिं रहीम कोउ लख्यो, गाढ़े दिन को मित्त ॥

M&R: 112: 80

With wealth, wife and offspring you are always occupied;
Why not seek a friend, Rahim, for trying times beside?

Rahim chides those who are constantly preoccupied with their own affairs. He reminds them that in times of misfortune, which may afflict one at any time, one needs friends. For, in difficult times, the immediate family is likely to be affected as well, and unable to assist. Another interpretation of this doha may well be that Rahim is asking us to be mindful about 'befriending' God, who is the most reliable of all in difficult times.

मथत-मथत माखन रहै, दही मही बिलगाय।
रहिमन सोई मीत है, भीर परे ठहराय ॥

M&R: 149: 84

Churning leaves butter behind, curd and buttermilk separate;
Rahim observes, a loyal friend stays put when the times are strait.

In the above doha Rahim reiterates a lesson he himself may have learnt: during times of sorrow and strife, only true friends stay with you. He illustrates this with a homely example: the churning of milk separates the buttermilk and leaves behind the most dense and valuable substance: butter.

रहीम अब वे बिरछ कहँ, जिनकी छाँह गंभीर।
बागन बिच-बिच देखियत, सेंहुड़, कुंज, करीर॥

M&R: 178: 87

Rahim asks, where are the trees whose shade is wide and deep?
Amidst gardens we now perceive clumps of thorny trees.

While Rahim seems to be lamenting the destruction of old trees, this doha appears to be entirely metaphorical. Perhaps he wrote it in his later years when his powerful, generous and reliable friends in high offices were gone and he was disenchanted by the younger men who had replaced them, since they were poorly disposed towards him.

रहिमन विपदा हू भली, जो थोरे दिन होय ।
हित अनहित या जगत में, जानि परत सब कोय ॥

M&R: 249: 95

Rahim, such hardships are useful that for short spells befall;
It is the good and evil times that expose one and all.

Paradoxical though the above doha may sound, Rahim is not asking us to wish affliction upon ourselves. The poet observes that it is useful to undergo misfortune for brief periods; such times reveal to us who our true friends are. Misfortune enables us to truly know the people around us.

On God

अमर बेलि बिनु मूल की, प्रतिपालत है ताहि ।
रहिमन ऐसे प्रभुहिं तजि, खोजत फिरिए काहि ॥

M&R: 10: 70

He rears even the immortal vine that thrives without roots;
Deserting such a Lord, Rahim, why should one cast about?

Amar Bel or Immortal Vine (*cuscuta europaea*) is a plant that has no roots but draws sustenance from the branches of trees it grows upon. Rahim says that even a plant without roots is nurtured by its maker. Why then, instead of recognising God's great mercy and generosity, and devoting themselves to Him, do most people travel to distant places and shrines in search of Him? Such an exercise is fruitless.

कहु रहीम कैसे बनै, अनहोनी ह्वै जाय।
मिला रहै औ ना मिलै, तासों कहा बसाय ॥

M&R: 36: 72

Rahim asks, how can it be? The unheard of befalls.
What we possess but cannot find, where do we install?

Addressing those who seek God in the manner of the Bhakti saint-poets, Rahim outlines the irony of their situation. People are unaware that God is within them and go around looking for Him and trying to establish His residence.

जेहि रहीम तन मन लियो, किियो हिए बिच भौन ।
तासों दुख सुख कहन की, रही बात अब कौन ॥

M&R: 72: 76

Rahim, He has my body and mind, in my heart resides;
Now what is left to tell Him of my sorrows and delights?

God is within us and knows all about our condition, our joys and sorrows. Therefore, Rahim asks, is there any point in constantly chanting His name? Here, Rahim appears to be challenging the Bhakti tenet of 'constantly taking God's name' to achieve *mukti*, freedom, from the cycle of birth, death and rebirth.

जो रहीम करिबे हुतो, ब्रज को इहै हवाल।
तौ काहे कर पर धरयौ, गोवर्धन गोपाल॥

M&R: 83: 77

If, Rahim, this is what you would do to the land of Braj,
Why then raise high Govardhan hill upon your palm, Gopal?

When Lord Indra, the god of thunder and rain, threatened Vrindavan with relentless rain, Krishna held up Govardhan hill above the people of Braj, to protect them and their livestock from being swept away. Rahim recalls this episode and gives voice to the reproach of the people of Braj, who ask Lord Krishna, 'If you had decided to forsake Vrinadvan and its people and go away to live in Dwarka, why did you save us from Indra's fury by holding aloft the mountain over us?'

हरि रहीम ऐसी करी, ज्यों कमान सर पूर।
खैंचि आपनी ओर को, डारि दियो पुनि दूर ॥

M&R: 286: 98

The Almighty treats Rahim like the bow treats the arrow: He draws him close towards Himself, then flings him far away.

It would appear that Rahim's fortunes were at an ebb when he wrote the above doha, for he does not hold back on his complaints against God. The warrior poet uses a martial metaphor to hint at His capricious behaviour. Just when God seems about to embrace him, He throws him far away, like an arrow shot by a soldier. Rahim feels aggrieved by such deceptive behaviour.

रहिमन बात अगम्य की, कहन सुनन को नाहिं ।
जो जानत ते कहत नाहिं, कहत ते जानत नाहिं ॥

M&R: 226: 92

Rahim, the unknowable isn't to be said or heard.
Those who know do not chatter, the ignorant hold forth.

It would appear that Rahim is referring to the ultimate knowledge of the Almighty in the Bhakti tradition. Wearied perhaps by the multitude who profess intimacy with God and preach about Him, he asks: how can we talk about God, who is unrecognisable through human faculties? And if we cannot fully understand the nature of the divine, why should we talk about it? We may know Him not through our senses but by experiencing Him through devotion. Those who do so cannot describe their feelings and keep quiet. Therefore, it is evident that those who speak about Him are ignorant of God.

It must be said there is no direct or indirect evidence to support this interpretation of the doha. It may apply equally to the knowledge of anything that is complex and difficult to grasp, but about which people are inclined to wax eloquent. Thus, the couplet may as easily be an injunction against ignorant speech.

On God's Grace

गहि सरनागति राम की, भवसागर की नाव।
रहिमन जगत उधार कर, और न कछू उपाय ॥

M&R: 51: 74

Seek refuge at the feet of Rama—ship of the worldly sea.
Rahim, besides this, from this world nothing can set you free.

Professing deep faith in Lord Krishna and Rama, Rahim exhorts us to take shelter at the feet of God. Without His blessings, we cannot safely cross the ocean of life and attain salvation.

धूर धरत निज सीस पै, कहु रहीम केहि काज ॥
जेहि रज मुनिपत्नी तरी, सो ढूँढ़त गजराज ॥

Bhati: 115: 130

Why does the elephant, asks Rahim, cover its
head with dust?
The elephant seeks the dust that freed Ahilya of the curse.

In a doha illustrative of Rahim's poetic imagination, he seeks to provide an explanation for a habit common among elephants. While walking along a path, from time to time, elephants pick up dust with their trunk and sprinkle it on their heads. Rahim first asks, why does the elephant do this? He then provides an explanation that recalls the story of Ahilya in the Ramayana. The deceitful Lord Indra seduces the sage Gautama's wife by disguising himself as the sage himself. The great sage curses Indra and turns his own wife into stone for her infidelity. Ahilya is eventually freed of the curse when Rama touches her with his feet.

रन, बन, ब्याधि, विपत्ति में, रहिमन मरै न रोय ।
जो रच्छक जननी-जठर, सो हरि गए कि सोय ॥

M&R: 174: 87

In war, woods, woe or mishap, Rahim, fear not death nor weep;
Your keeper in your mother's womb—has Hari gone to sleep?

Rahim urges the weak-hearted not to surrender to fear in any walk of life. He exhorts us to face whatever comes our way—whether in war or in a forest full of wild animals, in times of misery or misfortune—without fear. God, who looked after us in the most vulnerable period of our lives, when we were in our mother's womb, will take care of us. Therefore, we must give our best to life every day.

रहिमन को कोउ का करै, ज्वारी चोर लबार।
जो पति-राखनहार हैं, माखन-चाखनहार॥

M&R: 190: 88

What can they do to Rahiman—the gambler, thief or knave?
The guardian lord, Lover of Butter, is there to save.

Rahim was purportedly a devotee of Lord Krishna. Seemingly inspired by his faith, he states that no miscreant can harm him. He is confident that Krishna will come to save him if he is ever in danger. The doha is an instance of a devotee's faith in the butter-loving God.

रहीम बहु भेषज करत, ब्याधि न छाँड़त साथ।
खग मृग बसत अरोग बन, हरि अनाथ के नाथ॥

M&R: 225: 92

Despite many nostrums, Rahim, sickness won't let us be;
In healthful woods live birds and deer, God cares for the needy.

Although we have developed many medicines for the different types of ailments that assail us, humans have not been able to eliminate sickness; diseases continue to afflict all of us from time to time. Often, medicines do not bring relief, and when medicines fail, only God can come to our rescue. Indicating the birds and beasts that lead a healthy life inside the forests, Rahim seeks to reassure the poor that they may rely upon God to take care of them.

On Good Conduct

परि रहिबो मरिबो भलो, सहिबो कठिन कलेस ।
बामन है बलि को छल्यो, भलो दियो उपदेस ॥

M&R: 123: 81

I'd rather lie down and die or brook dire adversity
Than dupe Bali like the Dwarf after preaching charity.

The above doha reminds us of the story of Lord Vishnu's Vaman avatar, and how he dispossessed King Bali of his kingdom by duplicity (narrated earlier on p. 14). Reminding us of this episode, Rahim states that he would prefer death to Lord Vishnu's hypocrisy and deceit.

रहीम रिस को छाँड़ि कै, करौ गरीबी भेस।
मीठो बोलो नै चलो, सबै तुम्हारो देस॥

M&R: 242: 94

Rahim, first give up anger and then surrender pride;
The whole world is yours if you speak sweetly, are polite.

Rahim asks us to abjure two vices that could estrange us from others. If we wish to be at home wherever we go, we should first abandon anger and pride. We will then be able to speak sweetly, and such speech will endear us to all.

रहिमन अती न कीजिये, गहि रहिये निज कानि।
सैजन अति फूले तऊ डार पात की हानि॥

M&R: 175: 87

Rahim says, listen carefully, you must avoid excess;
If the morenga blooms too much, its boughs snap under stress.

The above doha warns us in no uncertain terms of the wages of excess. Even the health-giving morenga tree cannot escape the consequences of overabundance; its limbs break beneath the weight of its fruit. Thus, Rahim recommends moderation in everything.

फरजी साह न ह्वै सके, गति टेढी तासीर।
रहिमन सीधे चालसों, प्यादो होत वजीर॥

M&R: 131: 82

The queen cannot become king, by nature it's crooked;
Pawns get to be queen, Rahim, by moving straight ahead.

Rahim favours frankness and straightforwardness. Through this doha, Rahim suggests that frankness and straightforwardness help us to get ahead in this world. To illustrate his point, he draws our attention to the prospects of two pieces on the chessboard, the queen and the pawn. Since the queen can move in all directions and any number of squares, Rahim appears to suggest that it is easily manipulable, i.e., its principles are flexible; due to this flaw, the queen can never improve its position and become the king. On the other hand, the humble, literally straightforward pawn, by moving forward one square at a time, in a disciplined way, may reach the other end of the chessboard and thus be transformed into the queen.

On Greatness

जे गरीब पर हित करैं, तें रहीम बड़ लोग।
कहाँ सुदामा बापुरो, कृष्ण, मिताई जोग ॥

M&R: 68: 75

Those who befriend the poor, Rahim, are indeed great.
Or how could poor Sudama hope to be Krishna's mate?

Rahim says that those who help the poor are great. To illustrate, he recalls the friendship between Krishna and Sudama, as mentioned in the Bhagwat Purana. The two had grown up studying and playing together. However, their paths in life were different. Sudama, a poor Brahmin, grew up unable to shake off poverty while Krishna, the avatar of Vishnu, grew in stature.

Struggling with her circumstances, Sudama's wife, Susheela, suggested to him that he meet his powerful friend and seek his help. So, Sudama went off to see Krishna in Dwaraka, and as a gift he carried some beaten rice tied up in a small bundle.

Krishna was delighted to meet his old friend and embraced him. Awestruck by his palatial surroundings, Sudama hesitated to offer him his simple present and tried to hide the bundle. But the omniscient Lord Krishna snatched the bundle of beaten rice from him saying, 'That must be for me. Friend, give it to me,' and he began to eat the beaten rice with great enjoyment. When Sudama returned home after a few days, he found his decrepit hut transformed into a palace filled with riches.

जे रहीम बिधि बड़ किए, को कहि दूषन काढि ॥
चन्द्र दूबरो कूबरो, तऊ नखत तें बाढि ॥

M&R: 69: 76

Who can find any flaws, Rahim, in those made great by Fate?
The moon is brighter than the stars, although thin and curvate.

Tongue in cheek, Rahim points that though persons in high stations may have many flaws, these are invisible to people in general. Destiny raises such individuals so high that the world becomes blind to their faults. Rahim offers the example of the moon, which though bent and thin, outshines the distant stars; in other words, reflected glory often gains more in popular estimation than actual worth and distinction.

सीत हरत, तम हरत नित, भुवन भरत नहिं चूक ।
रहिमन तेहि रबि को कहा, जो घटि लखै उलूक ॥

M&R: 285: 98

He daily routs darkness and cold, and nourishes the earth:
What's it to the sun, Rahim, if the owl knows not his worth?

Without fail, every day, the sun shines on earth to free us of cold and darkness, and sustains life on the planet. It does not bother that the owl, which sleeps during the day and is about at night, is ignorant of its might and munificence. Rahim directs our attention to those who work selflessly to contribute to the betterment of society, whether their contributions are recognised or not. A person's worth, says Rahim, is independent of its recognition.

On Humility

छिमा बड़न को चाहिए, छोटेन को उतपात ।
का रहीमन हरि को घट्यो, जो भृगु मारी लात ॥

M&R: 59: 75

Forgiveness behoves elders, mischief becomes the youth.
When Bhrigu kicked him, Rahim asks, what did Hari lose?

In this doha Rahim points out the need for elders to be indulgent, or at least forgiving, of the indiscretions of the young and immature. Indeed, he indicates that those of greater stature—in age, wealth, power or prestige—are expected to be large-hearted and forgiving towards those who are less fortunate. He illustrates this by recalling an instance from the Puranas.

Rishi Bhrigu, son of Brahma, was called upon by other sages to decide who among the holy trinity of

Brahma, Vishnu and Shiva was the greatest. To test them, he decided to pay all three of them a visit. First, he walked up nonchalantly to his father. Brahma, seeing that his son did not greet him with the respect due to him, was angered and castigated him. Bhrigu, disappointed with his father's behaviour, went to Mount Kailash to meet Shiva. The ascetic god was delighted to see him and rushed to embrace him. Bhrigu, however, protested that Shiva was too dirty to be touched. Shiva flew into a rage and but for the intervention of Parvati would have slain the sage.

Finally, Bhrigu came to Vaikuntha, where he found Vishnu fast asleep on the coils of Sheshnaga. To wake him up, the sage kicked him on his chest. Springing up awake, a concerned Vishnu clutched Bhrigu's feet and asked him if he had hurt himself by striking his hard chest. Bhrigu then concluded that Vishnu was the greatest among the three gods since he alone had conquered anger.

देनहार कोउ और है, भेजत सो दिन रैन ।
लोग भरम हम पै धरें, याते नीचे नैन ॥

M&R: 109: 80

The benefactor is someone else who sends night and day;
Yet folks hold me responsible, therefore the lowered gaze.

Rahim was renowned for his generosity, and also for his humility. It came to be widely known that while giving alms to the poor and gifts to poets and writers, he would always lower his eyes. Puzzled by this, purportedly the poet Gang sent him a question in the form of a doha.[2] The above doha is Rahim's reply to Gang.

2 See Introduction, p. xxii.

रहिमन कबहुँ बड़ेन के, नाहिं गर्व को लेस।
भार धरैं संसार को, तउ कहावत सेस॥

M&R: 186: 88

Rahiman, those who are noble have not a trace of pride;
The world rests on Shesha's head, yet he's what 'remains behind'.

In Hindu mythology, Shesha, or Sheshanaga, is the king of serpents upon whose head rests the entire universe. Vishnu is often pictured as reclining on his bed of coils under his overspread hood. Despite his exalted position, Shesha is an ascetic. Recalling his humility, Rahim observes that those who are great are free of pride. Playing upon the word Shesha, which means 'remains behind' or 'remainder', Rahim points out that one who supports the world on his head is humble and flaunts no grand titles.

छोटेन सो सोहैं बड़े, कही रहीम यह रेख।
सहसन को हय बाँधियत, लै दमरी की मेख॥

M&R: 60: 75

Says Rahim, it's certain—the humble augment the great;
We tie a horse worth thousands to a two-paisa stake.

It is noteworthy that for the success of an exceptional enterprise or a valuable investment, often, something small becomes essential. For instance, although one may purchase a horse to ride that costs a fortune, to prevent it from wandering off, it has to be tied down to an inexpensive post stuck in the ground. All things large and minute have their place and use; their importance should not be underestimated. This doha recalls another on page 102.

धनि रहीम जल पंक को, लघु जिय पियत अघाय ।
उधदि बड़ाई कौन है, जगत पियासो जाय ॥

M&R: 114: 80

Rahim says, blessed is the slush where wee creatures slake their thirst.
What's so great about the ocean when the world is left athirst.

In this couplet Rahim highlights the importance of helping others in the smallest of ways. He applauds the muddy puddle while questioning the greatness of the ocean, for while the mud nurtures minuscule creatures, no one can quench their thirst by drinking sea water. In other words, even with limited resources, one may be able to make a large contribution to those in need of help.

रहिमन देखि बड़ेन को, लघु न दीजिये डारि ।
जहाँ काम आवे सुई, कहा करे तलवारि ॥

M&R: 211: 91

Impressed by powerful men, Rahim, don't spurn the feeble;
For what good is a broadsword when you require a needle?

In this doha Rahim warns us of the folly of estimating a person's worth based upon their station in life. He states that one should not be so impressed by the high and mighty that one begins to avoid those who are less powerful. We should remember that a button cannot be sewed on with a sword, only with a needle. Thus, every person is important in their own way.

On Love

कहि रहीम इक दीप तें, प्रगट सबै दुति होय ॥
तन सनेह कैसे दुरै, दृग दीपक जरु दोय ॥

M&R: 30: 72

Rahim, by the light of a lamp everything may be seen;
How can anybody hide love when two lamp-like eyes gleam?

Rahim contends in this doha that it is impossible to hide one's love for another. A single lamp dispels the darkness and illuminates everything in a room. Similarly, when two eyes light up on seeing someone, how can the person's love remain undiscovered? Love is irrepressible.

जाल परे जल जात बहि, तजि मीनन को मोह ।
रहिमन मछरी नीर को, तऊ न छांड़ति छोह ॥

M&R: 67: 75

Water eludes the net unmoved, it leaves the fish behind;
Even so for water, Rahim, the fish unswerving pine.

In this doha the poet speaks of unequal relationships. He compares the relationship between water and fish to that of lovers. He points out that the unfaithful water escapes the fisherman's net, abandoning the trapped fish to their fate; yet the fish never cease yearning for water. The fish are deeply attached to water, while the water appears to care nothing for them. Rahim suggests that this may be true of human beings too.

कहा करौं बैकुंठ लै, कल्प बृच्छ की छाँह ।
रहिमन ढाक सुहावनो, जो गल पीतम बाँह ॥

M&R: 40: 70

What will I do with heaven, the shade of
the Wishing Tree?
Rahiman, drums sound sweet with my lover's
arms around me.

Rahim says that he has no use for the distant heaven. Neither does he have so many wants that a Wishing Tree would be required to fulfil them. He is happiest in the company of his beloved; beyond that, he desires nothing. Thus, this doha focuses on the value of simple pleasures.

जे सुलगे ते बुझि गए, बुझे ते सुलगे नाहि ।
रहिमन दाहे प्रेम के, बुझि बुझि कै सुलगाहिं ॥

MSY: 66: 7

Whatever smoulders dies out, what's doused
won't burn again;
Rahim says, those charred by love blaze, again and again.

Reflecting on the nature of love, Rahim underlines its tenacity by comparing it to fire—one of the five essential elements. Any object that is touched by fire is destroyed; it turns to ashes. However, those who fall in love and are tormented by it cannot escape it. Instead of being extinguished, love is kindled again and again and the torment is unending. Thus, Rahim indicates that love is even more powerful than the fiercest of the five elements.

यह न रहीम सराहिए, लेन देन की प्रीति ।
प्रानन बाजी राखिए, हार होय कै जीति ॥

M&R: 266: 96

Says Rahim, do not praise love founded on give and take;
You may win or you may lose, but put your life at stake.

Rahim says that love dependent on transactions is not worthy of praise; the motive of gain cannot be its basis. Whether you win in love or lose, the only way is to stake all that you have on it, including your life.

रहिमन एक दिन वे रहे, बीच न सोहत हार।
वायु जु ऐसी बह गई, बीचन परे पहार॥

M&R: 183: 88

Rahim, there was a time a necklace couldn't come between us;
And now there blows such a breeze that mountains stand between us.

This is a lover's lament. Essentially, the lover reminds the beloved of a time when they were inseparable, but now, because of the cooling of ardour or a forced separation, they exist far apart.

रहिमन खोजे ऊख में, जहाँ रसन की खानि ।
जहाँ गाँठ तहँ रस नहीं, यही प्रीति में हानि ॥

M&R: 191: 89

Rahim examines sugarcane, seeking the store of juice;
In knots there is no sweetness—for love this is also true.

Scrutinising the length of a sugarcane, Rahim tries to identify exactly where the sap is concentrated. After the examination, he concludes that though the rest of the sugarcane is full of sweet juice, the knots in the cane do not contain any. He indicates that any kind of knot is bereft of sweetness, whether in sugarcane or in love.

This doha harks to the doha on the next page, in which Rahim warns us not to break the thread of love in haste, because once broken it cannot be joined without the impediment of a knot.

रहिमन धागा प्रेम का, मत तोड़ो चटकाय ।
टूटे से फिर ना मिले, मिले गाँठ परि जाय ॥

M&R: 212: 91

Rahiman, mind the thread of love do not hastily sever;
Once severed it will not join, save with a knot forever.

In one of his most popular dohas, Rahim cautions us against taking precipitous steps to end a relationship founded on love—be it with a lover, a friend or a relative. Breaking up with a loved one may be easy, but once ended, the relationship cannot return to the previous level of intimacy. The scar of the rupture will always be there to remind you of the incident. Therefore, in quarrels with loved ones, it is best not to take extreme actions.

बिरह रूप घन तम भयो, अवधि आस उद्योत।
ज्यों रहीम भादों निसा, चमकि जात खद्योत॥

M&R: 266: 96

In the gloom of separation hope shines a tiny light,
As glimmering fireflies, Rahim, illume a monsoon night.

The only bright spot in the gloom that shrouds the world of the beloved is hope. It is the hope of reunion with one's lover that gives one something to look forward to, just as on a monsoon night even the meagre light provided by fireflies can alleviate the darkness.

रहिमन प्रीति न कीजिये, जस खीरा ने कीन ।
ऊपर से तो दिल मिला, भीतर फाँकें तीन ॥

M&R: 220: 92

Rahim, don't be in love as the cucumber seems to be;
From outside its heart seems one, within it's split up in three.

Rahim says that the cucumber is a very poor example of love. Once the top is chopped off, it looks like its three parts are joined together. But that is only an illusion; they are actually separate. The message is that it is not enough for a group to appear cohesive. Individuals need to get past their differences and work together for their unity to be effective.

On Mortality

जैसी परै सो सहि रहै, कहि रहीम यह देह ।
धरती पर ही परत है, सीत घाम औ मेह ॥

M&R: 74: 76

Rahim, this body endures whatever comes its way,
For on earth alone descend hoarfrost, sun rays and rain.

Through the analogy of body and earth, Rahim affirms the mortality of human existence. He reminds us that human beings are of the earth and should expect and endure all that affects it—winter, summer and rain. The phrase 'धरती पर ही परत हैं' or 'on earth alone descend' seems to emphasise the point that as long as humans exist, they will experience natural phenomena that are beyond their control.

रहिमन ठठरी धूरि की, रही पवन ते पूरी।
गाँठ युक्ति की खुलि गई, अंत धूरि को धूरि॥

M&R: 204: 90

Rahiman, it is breath that makes this frame of clay robust;
Once the uniting knot unsnarls, all that remains is dust.

The body is made of earth and is made whole by breath or air. It is the bond between the five elements—earth, water, fire, wind and sky—that creates living beings. Once the knot holding the five elements becomes disentangled, all that remains of the body is dust. Thus, Rahim reminds us of the frailty of human beings.

भलो भयो धर तै छुट्यो, हँस्यो सीस परि खेत ।
काके-काके नवत हम, अपन पेट के हेत ॥

M&R: 143: 84

The severed head laughs in the field, 'Glad I'm finally free.
To how many I'd have to bow just to fill my belly!'

Rahim's message in the above doha is clear: a brave soldier would prefer to die on the battlefield rather than bow and scrape before the world to make a living. To him, self-respect is more important than his life.

सदा नगारा कूच का, बाजत आठों जाम।
रहिमन या जग आइ कै, को करि रहा मुकाम॥

M&R: 268: 97

On and on the marching drums beat on for ever and ever;
Who comes into this world, Rahim, to make a home forever?

Rahim posts a reminder to those who have come to believe and behave as if they will live forever. Time passes ceaselessly and ensures that change is the only constant. The doha recalls the line attributed to both Buddha and Jesus, as inscribed on the Buland Darwaza in Fatehpur Sikri: 'The world is a bridge, pass over it, but build no houses upon it. He who hopes for a day may hope for eternity; but the world endures but an hour.'

On the Path of Love

रहिमन पैंड़ा प्रेम को, निपट सिलसिली गैल ॥
बिछलत पाँव पिपीलिका, लोग लदावत बैल ॥

M&R: 222: 92

Rahim says, the path of love is a slippery track;
Though ants skid on it folks travel with laden bullocks!

Rahim warns those who are in love that their path passes through hazardous terrain where it is easy to slip and fall. He says that if even ants, who can go anywhere, find the path slippery, people who set off on it with a laden bullock are sure to fail. He indicates that those who wish to traverse the path of love successfully must be both surefooted and light on their feet. They must be focused on love alone and not carry any baggage from the past, or of expectations, which may throw them off balance.

रहिमन मैन-तुरंग चढ़ि, चलिबो पावक माँहि।
प्रेम-पन्थ ऐसो कठिन सबसों निबहत नाँहि॥

MSY: 217: 21

Rahim, astride a horse of wax, race through a field of fire:
The path of love is as trying, everyone can't aspire.

Rahim never tires of pointing out the tribulations faced by a lover. In this doha he states that the path of love passes through flames, which the lover must cross on a horse made of wax. The fiery challenge can only be navigated by a man of rare courage, skill and speed. Thus, the poet indicates the inevitability of lovers getting burnt in their attempt to find true love. It is interesting that 'मैन' in Brajbhasha has two meanings: 'wax' and 'Kamdeva', the God of love, even though Kamdeva's vehicle is not the horse but the parrot.

रहिमन मारग प्रेम को, मत मतिहीन मझाव ।
जो डिगिहै तो फिर कहूँ, नहिं धरने को पांव ॥

M&R: 230: 93

Rahim, the path of love is parlous, don't send fools along it.
If you stumble, there's no way to regain foothold upon it.

Rahim's advice to us is: please don't show fools the path of love. With the seeming authority of experience, he tells us that it is a narrow and dangerous track that requires clear thinking and balance. If you slip on it, you will not be able to get back on track.

On Poverty

कहि रहीम धन बढ़ि घटे, जात धनिन की बात ।
घटै बढै उनको कहा, घास बेंचि जे खात ॥

M&R: 31: 72

Rahim, wealth grows or wanes matters to the
well-off class;
What is more or less to those who live by selling grass?

Underscoring the vast difference between the perspectives of the rich and the poor, Rahim indicates that even the idea of improving one's fortunes is relative. Only those who possess wealth can meaningfully speak of its growth or decline. For, even the doubling of a poor person's possessions would still leave them indigent.

बरु रहीम कानन भलो, बास करिय फल भोग।
बंधु मध्य धनहीन ह्वै बसिबो उचित न योग॥

M&R: 263: 96

Rahim, better to dwell in woods and survive on fruits;
To live penniless amidst friends would not be astute.

This doha appears to belong to another low period of Rahim's life, when he was shorn of position and wealth. If one has fallen on hard times, it is better to move away to a place where one is unknown than to live upon the charity of friends. It would be preferable to lead a solitary life in the forest, subsisting on fruits, than to be among friends and constantly reminded of one's misery.

संपति भरम गँवाइ कै, हाथ रहत कछु नाहिं ।
ज्यों रहीम ससि रहत है, दिवस अकासहिं मांहि ॥

M&R: 282: 98

Once you lose the mirage of wealth, there's nothing to live by;
As in daytime, Rahim, the moon lies dully in the sky.

Rahim sounds a warning to those whose only goal in life is wealth. Once one realises that wealth is an illusion, one does not know what to aim or live for. One realises that wealth lacks any intrinsic merit, just as during the day the mundane moon, shorn of its borrowed radiance, is an unnoticed presence in the sky.

सर सूखे पच्छी उड़ै, औरे सरन समाहिं ॥
दीन मीन बिन पच्छ के, कहु रहीम कहँ जाहिं ॥

M&R: 276: 97

When lakes dry up, birds fly away to find
shelter elsewhere;
Rahim asks, without wings, can the poor fish
go anywhere?

Rahim contrasts the fate of fish, which are dependent on water for movement and life, with that of birds, which are dependent on their wings. He indicates that those who rely entirely upon others or are tied to external circumstances for their sustenance are vulnerable and may perish in times of change; those who depend upon themselves for their subsistence, are likely to adapt to a changing environment. Dependence only makes one vulnerable.

On Pride

जो रहीम ओछो बढ़ै, तौ अति ही इतराय ।
प्यादा सों फरजी भयो, टेढ़ो टेढ़ो जाय ॥

M&R: 82: 77

Rahim, as lowly men advance, they put on new airs;
When a pawn turns into queen, it only crosswise stirs.

Commenting on how circumstances affect human behaviour, Rahim says that when people in a low station of life are elevated to high positions, their demeanour changes dramatically. They affect superiority and pretend to graces that they have not grown into. In short, they are like pawns in a game of chess, which on reaching the opposite end of the chessboard and being transformed into the queen, instead of moving one square at a time, begin to race in all directions.

आप न काहू काम के, डार पात फल फूल ।
औरन को रोकत फिरैं, रहिमन पेड़ बबूल ॥

M&R: 15: 70

Its flowers and fruits are useless, so too its boughs and leaves;
The path of others too, Rahim, the babool tree impedes.

The babool tree is one that does not offer much by way of benefits; its flowers, fruit and wood are not of any use. Yet, it is full of pride and with its sharp thorns does its best to hinder the movement of humans and beasts. Drawing attention to these features of the tree, Rahim indicates that even if one is not in a position to contribute positively to society, the least one can do is to not hinder others.

बड़े बड़ाई ना करें, बड़े न बोलें बोल ।
रहिमन हीरा कब कहै, लाख टका है मोल ॥

M&R: 136: 86

The truly great never boast nor by tall claims entice;
Rahim, does a diamond claim, 'A million is my price'?

The above doha makes a simple point: those who are truly worthy of respect and admiration do not demand it or boast of their greatness. Rahim offers the example of a diamond whose worth is recognised by the viewer; the diamond does not make any claims of its own value.

On Prudence

अन्किन्हीं बातें करै, सोवत जागै जोय ।
ताहि सिखाय जगायबो, रहिमन उचित न होय ॥

M&R: 5: 69

Those who utter unseemly things and while awake who sleep,
To awaken them by teaching is not fitting, Rahim.

There is little point in trying to teach—or wake up—persons, who, knowing full well the implications (of their words and deeds), say or do unwarranted things. They are already conscious of their actions and are determined not to recognise the truth. Rahim says, let them be.

जैसी जाकी बुद्धि है, तैसी कहै बनाय ।
ताकों बुरा न मानिए, लेन कहाँ सो जाय ॥

M&R: 73: 76

As per their intelligence, people say what they know.
Do not mind them in the least, for where can
they get more?

Urging the virtue of patience, Rahim points out that people can only voice what their mind or intellect is capable of. Therefore, getting angry with them for saying something that is neither factually correct nor logical is futile; they know no better.

जो विषया संतन तजी, मूढ़ ताहि लपटाय ।
ज्यों नर डारत वमन कर, स्वान स्वाद सो खाय ॥

M&R: 92: 78

The evil that good folks spurn delights witless clods,
Just as what humans vomit is lapped up by dogs.

The distinction between the choices made by good persons and by rogues is highlighted in this doha. Rahim points out that those very things that the virtuous disapprove of, and reject, may delight people of weak intellect, just as dogs feast on the vomit of ailing humans.

रहिमन ब्याह बिआधि है, सकहु तो जाहु बचाय।
पायन बेड़ी परत हैं, ढोल बजाय बजाय॥

M&R: 224: 92

Marriage is a misfortune, Rahim, if you can, steer clear;
Your legs are put in shackles with revelry and fanfare.

Rahim warns the reader against marriage: it is a mishap into which one is tricked. According to the poet, while a person is distracted by the celebrations, their feet are being shackled and they become prisoners for ever.

रहिमन छोटे नरन सों, होत बड़ो नहीं काम ।
मढ़ो दमामो ना बने, सौ चूहे के चाम ॥

M&R: 196: 89

Little men, Rahim, cannot perform prodigious tasks:
A drum-skin can't be made from the skins of a hundred rats.

Rahim postulates that small-minded persons cannot do great deeds, just as a drumskin cannot be made with the skins of even a hundred rats. By 'little' men, Rahim is not referring to physical size but to vision, courage and ability—the hallmarks of the heroes of his time, be they warriors, statesmen, poets or kings. Meek persons with little ability and skill are unlikely to achieve anything great on the battlefield, in court or in public life—this is the message that the above doha imparts.

रहिमन रजनी ही भली, पिय सों होय मिलाप ।
खरो दिवस केहि काम जो, रहिबो आपुहि आप ॥

M&R: 237: 93

Rahim, night is preferable, for lovers may meet unknown.
What use is a brilliant day, if it leaves you all alone?

Rahim observes that a dark night is sometimes preferable to a bright day. For during the day, in the face of societal disapproval, lovers must keep to themselves and endure solitude. It is only at night that they may meet their beloved. Hence, Rahim votes for night over day. In sum, what appears to not benefit one person may offer unexpected advantages to another.

On Sorrow

अन्तर दाव लगी रहै, घुआँ न प्रगटै सोइ ।
कै जिय आपन जानहीं, कै जिहि बीती होइ ॥

M&R: 4: 69

Although fires may blaze within, there is no sign of smoke.
Who can know what is inside save they who bear the yoke?

Speaking of the difference between appearance and reality, Rahim observes that although a person may be in deep torment their feelings may not reflect on their visage. No one can truly guess what goes on within another's heart. Only someone in a smilar situation can truly understand its cause and intensity. As Shakespeare put it, 'Every man can bear a grief save he who has it.'

होत कृपा जो बड़ेन की, सो कदाचि घटि जाय ।
तौ रहीम मरिबो भलो, यह दुख सहो न जाय ॥

M&R: 289: 99

If of elders' blessings one is suddenly bereft,
It's better to die, Rahim, this grief one can't accept.

It is tempting to conclude from the above doha that Rahim is grieving the demise of Akbar, his emperor and guardian. After Bairam Khan's murder in Patan, Akbar had taken the fatherless four-year-old under his guardianship. Rahim had progressed steadily and earned the emperor's trust, regard *and* affection. However, there is no evidence to indicate that Rahim is indeed grieving Akbar's demise with this doha.

रहिमन निज मन की विथा, मन ही राखो गोय ।
सुनि अठिलैहैं लोग सब, बाँटि न लैहैं कोय ॥

M&R: 214: 91

Rahim warns, lock up your grief within your heart. Beware!
If folks find out they'll just sneer, not one of them will share.

Most people around you do not care for your grief. Indeed, they are likely either to play it down and ridicule it or even derive satisfaction from your ill-luck. Therefore, Rahim advises, there is little profit in sharing one's woes with others; it is best to keep quiet and hold them in one's heart.

माह मास लहि टेसुआ, मीन परे थल और।
त्यों रहीम जग जानिए, छुटे आपुने ठौर॥

M&R: 159: 85

Like bare tesu trees in winter or fish stranded on sand
Are they in this world, Rahim, who have left behind their land.

To Rahim, being divorced from his land was a matter of great sorrow. He likened the lives of people in such a predicament as being empty of beauty, like leafless tesu trees or fish out of water.

On Speech

अधम बचन काको फल्यो, बैठि ताड़ की छाँह ।
रहिमन काम न आय है, ये नीरस जग माँह ॥

M&R: 3: 69

Who has gained from false words or resting in the palm tree's shade?
In this colourless world, Rahim, they don't come to your aid.

Believing that impious or false words will fetch us dividends is akin to seeking rest in the shade of a tall, thin palm tree. Here, false words may represent unrealistic hopes or false promises while the palm tree may stand for a weak and unreliable friend or patron. Neither is any use in this transactional world. Rahim implies here that only truth and capable allies may be relied upon in life.

खीरा सिर तें काटिए, मलियत नमक लगाय।
रहीम करुए मुखन को, चहिअत इहै सजाय ॥

M&R: 47: 73

Slice the cucumber at the top and rub salt upon it;
This is the punishment, Rahim, that nasty mouths merit.

Traditionally, in India, to extract the bitterness from a cucumber, we slice off the top, sprinkle salt on it, and then rub the two pieces together. Rahim suggests that there will be people who contribute bitterness to our life. To elicit good behaviour from them, they too should be treated with severity.

रहिमन जिह्वा बावरी, कहि गइ सरग पाताल ।
आपु तो कहि भीतर रही, जूती खात कपाल ॥

M&R: 201: 90

Rahim, the tongue is mad, it prattles of heaven and hell;
Then it keeps inside the mouth, shoes land on the head pell-mell.

Unless you control your tongue, you may get into trouble. Unless guided by the mind and good sense, the tongue, like a lunatic, is capable of uttering anything, about anything, ranging from the depths of hell to the heights of heaven. However, the consequences will be suffered by the head, which is held responsible for the foolish pronouncements of the tongue. In short, think before you speak.

On Time

ऊगत जाही किरण सों, अथवत ताही काँति ।
त्यौं रहीम सुख दुख सबै, बढ़त एक ही भाँति ॥

M&R: 18: 70

The rays that grace the rising sun with sunset fade away;
Akin, Rahim, to joy and grief, both grow in the same way.

The glorious diurnal journey of the sun begins with the rays that appear on the horizon, while the last rays of the setting sun mark the end of its glory. Rahim reminds us that both joy and grief in human life grow and wane, just like the sun. We should neither set store by joyous events, nor be dismayed by grief; both will pass.

यह रहीम निज संग लै, जनमत जगत न कोय ।
बैर प्रीति अभ्यास जस, होत होत ही होय ॥

M&R: 166: 86

Rahim says, no one is born into this world with these:
Ill will, love, practice and fame—all, by and by, increase.

Human beings are not born with the things that matter in life; both negative and positive accomplishments, of necessity, take time. One cannot acquire either the ill-will or love of others in a flash. Similarly, abilities and accomplishments that require practice and fame do not accrue to anyone overnight. They can be acquired only with time and persistence.

रहिमन असमय के परे, हित अनहित ह्वै जाय ।
बधिक बधै मृग बानसों, रुधिरै देत बताय ॥

M&R: 179: 87

Rahim, in adverse times what's good also becomes a bane;
The hunter's arrow hits its mark—discloses the bloodstain.

On the theme of Fate, Rahim observes that when the stars are against you, that which is intrinsically beneficial may prove to be your undoing. For instance, after being wounded by a hunter's arrow, a deer may escape and lie low in the grass. Yet, the trail of blood left behind by it reveals his hiding place to the hunter. Thus, blood that is essential to life can also become the betrayer of life.

रहिमन चुप ह्वै बैठिए, देखि दिनन को फेर ।
जब नीके दिन आइ हैं, बनत न लगि है देर ॥

M&R: 8: 69

Rahim, sit quietly and observe the days turn;
It won't take long to make good when the good times return.

Rahim's advice to those facing difficult circumstances is to wait and watch. Instead of worrying or struggling against the tide, they should let the hard times pass, for they are sure to be successful in their ventures when circumstances improve. While highlighting the fluctuations of fate, this doha also tells us to have patience, since the wheel of time is bound to turn full circle.

रहिमन जग जीवन बड़े, काहु न देखे नैन ।
जाये दशानन अछत ही, कपि लागे गथ लैन ॥

M&R: 198: 89

Rahim, in this world and life none is great forever;
As soon as mighty Ravana fell, monkeys sacked his treasure.

Repeating an often voiced warning against the sin of pride, Rahim here recalls the lot of Ravana, the mighty king of Lanka, in the Ramayana. Although a learned man with many spiritual and temporal achievements, Ravana's pride prompted him to challenge Lord Rama. Inevitably, Ravana was defeated on the battlefield and killed. No sooner was his army routed that Rama's army of monkeys took over his kingdom and his treasury. Pride, indeed, comes before a fall.

रूप, कथा, पद, चारु पट, कंचन, दोहा, लाल।
ज्यों-ज्यों निरखत सूक्ष्म गति, मोल रहीम बिसाल॥

M&R: 257: 95

Beauty, parable, verse, fine clothes, rubies, couplets and gold—
As you slowly examine each, its worth grows manifold.

There are many objects whose worth may be gauged at first sight. But there are a few things whose value dawns upon us gradually. The more closely one looks at a lovely face, a parable, a hymn, fine clothes, gold, dohas and rubies, newer facets and shades of meaning are revealed, thereby increasing the value of each. In sum, it takes time and a fine eye to appreciate the value of some of the most precious things around us.

बहै प्रीति नहिं रीति वह, नहीं पाछिलो हेत।
घटत-घटत रहिमन घटै, ज्यों कर लीन्हें रेत॥

M&R: 264: 96

Neither affection nor custom, nor does past love subsist;
They dwindle steadily, Rahim—as sand runs through the fist.

The context of the above doha is not clear. In a melancholy mood, Rahim appears to bemoan the inevitable waning of love and affection with the passing of time, and even of the practices or interactions that were once strengthened by love.

समय पाय फल होत है, समय पाय झरि जाय ।
सदा रहै नहीं एक सी, का रहीम पछिताय ॥

M&R: 273: 97

The tree bears fruit in its own time, with time it also falls;
Time is never the same, Rahim, why regret what befalls?

Apparently composed during one of the low periods of Rahim's life, the above doha advises us to accept the ever-changing cyclical nature of life. A tree may bear sweet fruits when the time is appropriate, but, when these fruits become overripe, they fall to the ground. Then, again, only leaves remain on the trees until it is time for them to flower. Since this pattern is unceasing, one must accept it and come to terms with both, the bounteous and the barren periods in one's life.

समय लाभ सम लाभ नहिं, समय चूक सम चूक ।
चतुरन चित रहिमन लगी, समय चूक की हूक ॥

M&R: 274: 97

There is no gain like time gained, no loss like lost time.
The wise deeply feel, Rahim, the cost of lost time.

Underscoring the significance of time, Rahim indicates that it is more valuable than anything else because it cannot be substituted. Time is 'gained' by utilising it; it is 'lost' if it is not used gainfully. Only wise persons appreciate the value of time. In other words, understanding the worth of time and acting upon it is wisdom.

On Wealth

बढ़त रहीम धनाढ्य धन, धनौ धनी को जाइ।
धटै बढ़ै वाको कहा, भीख मांगि जो खाइ॥

M&R: 137: 83

Rahim says, the rich grow richer, wealth flows to the wealthy.
What is rise and fall to them who beg to fill their belly?

Rahim points out that, almost routinely, wealth accrues where it already exists; the wealthy also have the wherewithal to increase their fortune. The poor do not have to worry about whether their net worth is increasing or decreasing; their principal worry is the next meal. Thus, Rahim highlights the ironical fate of the wealthy—those who need worry least about their material condition are the ones incessantly preoccupied with the state of their fortune.

बिपति भए धन ना रहे, रहे जो लाख करोर ।
नभ तारे छिपि जात हैं, ज्यों रहीम भए भोर ॥

M&R: 141: 83

Although you may have billions, in crises wealth doesn't stay;
Rahim remarks, when the day dawns the stars all fade away.

In the above doha Rahim underlines the limitations of wealth. Money cannot guarantee relief from misfortunes. The intensity of a disaster may well make it appear inconsequential, just as at dawn, the stars, though still in the firmament, not only stop shining but for all practical purposes, cease to exist.

रहिमन वित्त अधर्म को, जरत न लागै बार ।
चोरी करि होरी रची, भई तनिक में छार ॥

M&R: 247: 95

Rahim, the wealth of wicked folk is burnt up in a flash;
If you steal to celebrate Holi, money turns to ash.

Rahim points out that wealth acquired through immoral and illegal means does not last long. He offers an analogy from the festival of colours, Holi.

Hiranyakashyapu, the lord of the monsters, unhappy that his young son Prahalad was devoted to God, asked his daughter to get rid of her brother. The deceitful Holika tried to kill her pious brother by sitting with him on a funeral pyre, but with a magical protective sheet around her own shoulders. As the flames leapt up, by God's grace, the sheet slipped off her shoulders and fell on Prahalad; Holika was devoured by the flames but Prahalad escaped unharmed.

In the weeks preceding Holi, young boys in villages go around collecting wood for the bonfires they will build on the eve of the spring festival, in remembrance of the devotion of Prahalad. Most of this wood is stolen from gardens and plantations and is quickly consumed by the flames.

On Wise Conduct

काह कामरी पामरी, जाड़ गए से काज।
रहिमन भूख बुताइए, कैस्यो मिलै अनाज ॥

M&R: 41: 73

What of blankets of silk or wool, so long the cold keeps out?
What matters what you eat, Rahim, if your hunger is doused?

In this couplet Rahim indicates the folly of losing sight of one's basic needs. He illustrates his point with two examples that would be familiar to all of us—the need to stay warm in winter and to eat one's fill. How luxurious the rug is, and whether it is made of pure wool or fine silk, is immaterial; it should keep one warm. Similarly, the kind of food you eat is secondary as long as there is enough to satiate one's hunger.

यों रहीम सुख दुःख सहत, बड़े लोग सह साँति।
उवत चन्द जेहि भांति सो, अथवत ताहि भांति॥

M&R: 173: 87

Rahim remarks, great folk stay both in joy and grief serene;
The setting moon looks just the same as when it first is seen.

In this doha, perhaps written during a trying period of his life, Rahim tells us—and maybe himself—that it is best to remain unmoved by either happiness or distress, since one is likely to follow the other. He points to the moon that is materially unaffected by either night or day. A cynosure of all eyes through the night, it passes unnoticed during the daylight hours. Yet, from the beginning to the end, its form remains unchanged.

रहिमन अँसुआ नैन ढरि, जिय दुख प्रगट करेइ।
जाहि निकारो गेह ते, कस न भेद कहि देइ॥

M&R: 180: 87

Tears flowing from the eyes, Rahim, bare the pain in the heart.
Those you cast out of your house, why won't they with secrets part?

In the above doha Rahim tells us to be careful of what we reveal. Tears are usually the sign of sorrow; if people see you crying, they are sure to grasp that you are unhappy. Similarly, if you turn out a worker from your home, they are sure to tell the world your secrets. Rahim indicates that one should be careful with one's expressions in public, as well as how one treats those in one's employ.

रहिमन कठिन चितान तें, चिंता को चित चेत।
चिता दहति निर्जीव को, चिंता जीव समेत॥

M&R: 185: 88

More than funeral pyres, Rahim, beware of worrying;
Pyres incinerate the dead but worries scorch the living.

Rahim's advice to those who are occupied with thoughts of death and funerals is to stop worrying. He points out that a cremation pyre performs the necessary function of reducing a lifeless body to ashes; however, a person given to worrying attracts ailments that work to wreck their body and mind.

रहिमन तब लगि ठहरिए, दान मान, सनमान ।
घटत मान देखिय जबहिं, तुरतहि करिय पयान ॥

M&R: 205: 90

Says Rahim, remain a guest till warmth and
welcome last;
When you perceive respect decline, clear out of there fast.

The above doha espouses a principle of social intercourse. One should stay as a guest with a friend or a relative only for as long as their hospitality is of a high order. The moment their treatment of you flags, it is best to bid the host goodbye. In short, do not overstay your welcome

रहिमन निज संपति बिना, कोउ न बिपति सहाय ॥
बिनु पानी ज्यों जलज को, नहिं रवि सकै बचाय ॥

M&R: 215: 91

Rahim, if you're poor, none will ease your misery;
Without water, the sun can't save the water-lily.

Rahim points out that no one will come to your aid in hard times, unless you have sufficient reserves of your own. Even the all-powerful sun cannot revive the stricken water-lily, unless there is water around it. In a crisis, one must be able to rely upon one's own resources.

रहिमन पानी राखिए, बिनु पानी सब सून ।
पानी गए न ऊबरै, मोती मानुष चून ॥

M&R: 219: 92

Save water, Rahim, without water nought survives:
Pearls, humans, or quicklime, sans water cannot thrive.

Rahim urges us to conserve water, without which there can be no life. Nothing can grow or be of use without water—be it pearls in the ocean, humans on earth or quicklime, which softens and swells up to mix well with water, and then is used to whitewash walls.

भीत गिरी पाखान की, अररानी वहि ठाम ॥
अब रहीम धोखो यहै, को लागै केहि काम ॥

M&R: 147: 84

The stone wall fell down with a crash where it had stood before;
Rahim asks, can anyone now say where each stone will go?

Through the metaphor of a stone wall, Rahim explains the relationship between individuals and the organisation or the society to which they belong. As long as an individual is part of a larger scheme or system, their life is meaningful and valuable; once the larger scheme itself is in disarray, the individual also loses identity and purpose. As long as the brick wall stands, all the bricks serve their individual purpose. Once the wall falls, the stones are scattered and rendered unusable. The utility of the individual stone blocks, as well as of the erstwhile wall, dissolve simultaneously.

रहिमन विद्या बुद्धि नहिं, नहीं धरम जसदान ।
भू पर जनम वृथा धरै, पसु बिनु पूँछ विषान ॥

M&R: 248: 95

Says Rahim, without wit, learning, charity, faith, or fame
One is a beast sans horns and tail, born upon Earth in vain.

Rahim states that human life is special and we should strive to make it worthwhile. In a lifetime, a person should acquire one or more marks of distinction: they may acquire knowledge, share what they are fortunate to have with others, learn to have faith in the Almighty, apply their mind to resolving problems or earn fame. If a person does not have any of these qualities, they are akin to sheep—an animal without horns or tail, i.e., any marks of distinction.

रहिमन राज सराहिए, ससिसम सुखद जो होय।
कहा बापुरो भानु है, तपै तरैयन खोय।

M&R: 240: 94

Rahim, applaud the reign that like the moon makes you serene;
What use is the poor blazing sun, the stars just flee the scene.

Probably scorched by the Emperor's wrath, Rahim states that a sovereign's reign should be like the soothing rays of the moon shining in the night sky, surrounded by stars. What good can come of an emperor who is forever blazing with anger? Like the sun, whose arrival at dawn drives away the stars, when such a monarch appears, his courtiers keep out of sight.

रोल बिगाड़े राज नै, मोल बिगाड़े माल ॥
सनै सनै सरदार की, चुगल बिगाड़े चाल ॥

M&R: 259: 96

Kings spoil the rule of law while traders ruin trade,
And, bit by bit, backbiting blights the leader's ways.

Rahim states that kings themselves are responsible for vitiating the rule of law, while traders often harm their own trade. It is those who fawn around a leader, filling his ears with spiteful talk and poisoning his mind against good people, who end up misleading him.

On Worldly Conduct

अब रहीम मुश्किल पड़ी, गाढ़े दोऊ काम ।
साँचे से तो जग नहीं, झूठे मिलैं न राम ॥

M&R: 9: 69

Now, Rahim, you're in trouble: both choices are hard;
Truth does not yield this world and lies don't win you God.

In this doha Rahim presents a fundamental dilemma that we often face. In life, there are two paths—the path of truth and the path of untruth. According to Rahim, truth leads to God, while abandoning it for untruth usually secures success in the corporeal world. Since opting for one excludes the other, it is a difficult choice to make. In sum, Rahim implies that we may choose either material success or spiritual fulfilment—not both.

असमय परे रहीम कहि, माँगि जात तजि लाज।
ज्यों लछमन माँगन गए, पारासर के नाज॥

M&R: 13: 70

In adverse times, Rahim, you may beg without any shame;
As Lakshman went to Parashar to ask him for some grain.

When misfortune afflicts a person, they may abandon shame and be driven to beg for help. Rahim believes that this is understandable; since there is no other alternative for survival, even begging for help is acceptable. As a case in point, he highlights an incident from the Ramayana. When Rama, Sita and Lakshmana were banished from Ayodhya, Lakshman was unable to find any food in the forest for Rama and Sita. Coming upon the ashram of the sage Parashara, he did not hesitate to beg for food so that his brother and sister-in-law would not go hungry.

कैसे निबहैं निबल जन, करि सबलन सों गैर ।
रहिमन बसि सागर बिषे, करत मगर सों वैर ॥

M&R: 43: 73

How can weak folk get by if they turn mighty
men hostile?
Those who live in water, Rahim, daren't cross
the crocodile.

Rahim cautions that if one wishes to survive in society, one cannot make enemies of powerful people. Not only can such people deny help to the poor but, if angered, may also harm them.

गगन चढ़ै फिर क्यों तिरै, रहिमन बहरी बाज।
फेरि आई बन्धन परै, पेट अधम के काज ॥

Bhati: 49: 108

Why does the deaf falcon, Rahim, return after soaring high?
It comes back to bondage because with base hunger is the tie.

Rahim poses a question: why does the captive falcon, once released by the falconer and able to fly into the firmament unhindered, come back to its captor despite being deaf to commands? Why does it not fly away to freedom? The poet answers his own question: it is a matter of filling the belly. The falcon has become used to being supplied with food and has become dependent on it; for the sake of its stomach, it has bartered its independence. Rahim indicates that this is often true for humans too.

रहिमन जो रहिबो चहै, कहै वाहि के दाँव।
जो बासर को निस कहै, तौ कचपची दिखाव॥

M&R: 203: 90

Rahim, if you'd be in with them, agree with what they say;
If they declare that day is night, point out the Milky Way.

In this doha Rahim offers advice tongue-in-cheek to those who wish to rise in life, and in court, at any cost. If they wish to be in the good books of their superior or an influential person, they must agree enthusiastically with whatever they say. Thus, during the day, if their superior says it is night, they must immediately point to the Milky Way in the sky. Thus, Rahim illustrates how absurd flatterers can be while trying to please their masters.

समय परे ओछे बचन, सबके सहै रहीम।
सभा दुसासन पट गहे, गदा लिए रहे भीम॥

M&R: 272: 97

In hard times we must bear, Rahim, all the abuse we face;
While Duhshasan pulled the sari, Bhim stood holding his mace.

In the Mahabharata, Yudhishthira, the eldest of the Pandava brothers, lost to Duryodhan, the eldest of the Kauravas, in the infamous game of dice. Not only did he lose all their assets, including wealth and property, but also Draupadi, their wife. When Dushasan, one of the Kaurava brothers, began to disrobe Draupadi in the middle of the assembly to further humiliate the Pandavas, even Bhim, the strongest of warriors, was unable to intervene, shackled as he was by the rules of the game.

Thus, Rahim reminds us that however powerful a person may be, he has to bear the embarrassment and disgrace that falls to his lot during times of misfortune.

सौदा करो सो करि चलौ । रहिमन याहि बाट ॥
फिर सौदा पैहौ नहीं । दूरि जान है बाट ॥

M&R: 280: 98

Trade if you wish to as you go, Rahim, this is the path;
After this you won't get a chance, the road goes very far.

Rahim says that our life is like a trade route, and as we traverse it, we should buy and sell wisely without wasting time. We should invest keeping in mind that the journey meanders well beyond our present life, and the final account of profit and loss will be made at its end.

Bibliography

Bhati, Deshraj Singh (ed.). *Rahim Granthavali*. New Delhi: Naman Prakashan, 2011.

Busch, Allison. *Poetry of Kings: The Classical Hindi Literature of Mughal India*. New Delhi: Permanent Black, 2022.

Busch, Allison. 'Life and Love in the Couplets of Rahim' in Hussain, Shakeel & Ray, Deeti (eds). *Celebrating Abdul Rahim Khan-i-Khana: Statesman, Courtier, Soldier, Poet, Linguist, Humanitarian, Patron*. Ahmedabad: Mapin Publishing, 2017.

Chander Shekhar. 'From the Pen of Abdur Rahim Khan-i-Khana' in Hussain, Shakeel & Ray, Deeti (eds). *Celebrating Abdul Rahim Khan-i-Khana: Statesman, Courtier, Soldier, Poet, Linguist, Humanitarian, Patron*. Ahmedabad: Mapin Publishing, 2017.

Devi Prasad, Munshi. *Khanakhanan Nama*, edited by Jaswant Singh. New Delhi: Rupa Publications, 2006.

Hawley, John Stratton. 'Foreword' in Sinha, Chandan. *The Vision of Wisdom, Kabir: Selected Sakhis*. New Delhi: Rupa Publications, 2020.

Lefèvre, Corrinne. 'The Court of Abd-ur-Rahim Khan-i-Khanan as a Bridge Between Iranian and Indian Cultural Traditions' in Bruijn, Thomas de and Busch, Allison (eds). *Culture and Circulation: Literature in Motion in Early Modern India*. The Netherlands: Brill, 2014.

Mishra, Vidyaniwas and Rajneesh, Govind (eds). *Rahim Granthavali*. New Delhi: Zenith Publishers, 2005.

Orthmann, Eva. 'The Donor Is Someone Else' in Hussain, Shakeel & Ray, Deeti (eds). *Celebrating Abdul Rahim Khan-i-Khana: Statesman, Courtier, Soldier, Poet, Linguist, Humanitarian, Patron*. Ahmedabad: Mapin Publishing, 2017.

Pandey, Manager. 'Sanskritik Sangam ke Kavi Rahim' in Trivedi, Harish & Ray, Deeti (eds). *Abdur-Rahim Khanekhana: Kavya Saoundarya aur Sarthakta*. New Delhi: Vani Prakashan, 2019.

Raghavan, T.C.A. *Attendant Lords: Bairam Khan and Abdur Rahim, Courtiers & Poets in Mughal India*. New Delhi: HarperCollins Publishers, 2017.

Russel, Ralph (ed.). *The Oxford India Ghalib: Life, Letters and Ghazals*. New Delhi: Oxford University Press, 2011.

Sharma, Sunil. 'Nihavandi on Rahim' in Hussain, Shakeel & Ray, Deeti (eds). *Celebrating Abdul Rahim Khan-i-Khana: Statesman, Courtier, Soldier, Poet, Linguist,*

Humanitarian, Patron. Ahmedabad: Mapin Publishing, 2017.

Siddiqui, Iqtidar Hussain. 'Abdur Rahim Khan-i-Khana: A Biographical Note' in Hussain, Shakeel & Ray, Deeti (eds). *Celebrating Abdul Rahim Khan-i-Khana: Statesman, Courtier, Soldier, Poet, Linguist, Humanitarian, Patron*. Ahmedabad: Mapin Publishing, 2017.

Snell, Rupert. 'Briefly Put: Rahim's Barvai Couplets' in Hussain, Shakeel & Ray, Deeti (eds). *Celebrating Abdul Rahim Khan-i-Khana: Statesman, Courtier, Soldier, Poet, Linguist, Humanitarian, Patron*. Ahmedabad: Mapin Publishing, 2017.

Trivedi, Harish. 'Rahim in His World and in Ours' in Hussain, Shakeel & Ray, Deeti (eds). *Celebrating Abdul Rahim Khan-i-Khana: Statesman, Courtier, Soldier, Poet, Linguist, Humanitarian, Patron*. Ahmedabad: Mapin Publishing, 2017.

Trivedi, Harish. 'Rahim—Parichay evam Paricharcha' in Trivedi, Harish & Ray, Deeti (eds). *Abdur-Rahim Khanekhana: Kavya Saoundarya aur Sarthakta*. New Delhi: Vani Prakashan, 2019a.

Trivedi, Harish. 'Rahim ki Jeevan Drishti' in Trivedi, Harish & Ray, Deeti (eds). *Abdur-Rahim Khanekhana: Kavya Saoundarya aur Sarthakta*. New Delhi: Vani Prakashan, 2019b.

Truschke, Audrey. 'Indo-Persian Translations'. *Seminar* No. 671, 2015. https://www.india-seminar.com/2015/671/671_audrey_truschke.htm. Accessesd on 31/07/2015 at 08:37 a.m.

Yajnik, Mayashankar (ed). *Rahim Ratnavali*. Kashi: Sahitya Seva Sadan, 1928.

Index of first-half of first lines – Hindi (Devanagari)

Index of first-half of first lines – English

Acknowledgements

I began translating Rahim's dohas along with Kabir's sakhis in 2009–10. Within a couple of years, as I delved deeper into both, I realised that I needed to concentrate on one. I chose Kabir first and set aside Rahim for the time being. *The Vision of Wisdom, Kabir: Selected Sakhis* was published in October 2020 in the middle of the Covid pandemic. As I resumed work on Rahim's dohas, *Kabir*'s reception affirmed my belief that translation of Hindi verse in metre and rhyme, as obtains in the original, is the right way forward.

Prof. Harish Trivedi, my former teacher and an authority on both translation studies and Rahim, has been a constant source of encouragement. Over the years, he went through several sets of translations of Rahim's dohas that I sent him; his response was most heartening. Also, his intermittent queries on the progress of work indicated his interest not only in Rahim but also in my translations, for which I am grateful.

Prof. Purushottam Agrawal, who had earlier gone through the manuscript of *The Vision of Wisdom, Kabir: Selected Sakhis*, very kindly agreed to write the Foreword for this book. I am indebted to him not only for his uplifting assessment of the book, but also for underlining the problems of translating verse more than five centuries old while preserving its integrity.

In the course of writing this book I also received encouragement from Shri Binod Kumar, Prof. Jack Hawley and Dr Shashank Shekhar Sinha. As before, Shri Randhir Arora has given generously of his time and advice. Ms Aparna Kumar provided valuable feedback on the manuscript and practical suggestions. My warm thanks are due to each of them.

To the meticulous team at Westland I owe a special word of thanks. To both Ms V.K. Karthika and Ms Ajitha G.S., the editors, I owe deep appreciation for their diligence and patience in working long hours with me to turn a manuscript into a book.

My wife, Nandita, is the mainstay of my writing—the first reader, listener and critic. Neilabh, our son, researched and shared with me references and articles on Rahim and his times. Our daughter, Vedushi, has designed the beautiful cover of this book, reflecting the richness of Rahim's poetry—just as she designed the cover of *The Vision of Wisdom, Kabir: Selected Sakhis*. And my mother blesses me daily. I am grateful to all of them for sustaining me.